To Love Another Person

A Spiritual Journey Through Les Miserables

John Morrison

D1452636

To Love Another Person

Zossima Press books are designed in Cheshire, Connecticut
and may be purchased for business or promotional use or special sales.

Zossima
Press

ISBN 0-9723221-9-1

ISBN-13 9780972322195

DEDICATION

For Susan, Tom, and Nina

Table of Contents

PREFACE

In 1987, having prepared ourselves by listening to the tape recording several times, my wife and I went to see *"Les Miserables"* on Broadway. After "One Day More," the rousing finale to the first act, Susan said to me that "it can't get any better than this." But it did and the ride home was spent recalling the excellences of the production, rejoicing in the power of the story and the music as they evoked awed responses from an audience which had engaged itself on multiple levels with Jean Valjean's journey to salvation.

We knew that more was at work than merely a thrilling night at the theater, but at the moment we were at a loss to articulate what the more was after such an intense encounter. An inner voice was sounding and it announced a need for engagement. We had been moved by the music and the words, by the great themes of passion and pain, love and redemption, but also with the sense that there was something special, something elusive. So we returned, obedient to the voice, looking for that elusive something and certain that it, whatever it was, could not be reduced to Jean Valjean, Fantine, and Eponine's sublime final line, "to love another person is to see the face of God." How to define the dynamism of the musical could be ascertained only by a journey through the novel, by a willingness to acknowledge the source.

Having read an abridged edition of Hugo's work when I was fourteen and a freshman in high school, having encountered "The

Bishop's Candlesticks" in anthologies where it masqueraded as a short story, and having followed Richard Kimball's flight from Inspector Girard in television's "The Fugitive," I was familiar with the essential plot of *Les Miserables*. However, forty years and an immature early reading imposed a distance from the original that had to be bridged. So it was back to the novel, the Penguin edition translated by Norman Denny, and to the discovery that this *chef d'oeuvre* transcended the nineteenth century and that the musical was securely anchored in it, that the theatrical production enhanced the power of its source without ever rendering that source trivial.

The consequence of this discovery was a passionate desire to expose my students to this drama of salvation, to this tale of one man's journey toward freedom and glory, without imposing arbitrarily on them the works' ideas. Each year I would re-read the book, teach it in conjunction with the musical, and then bring my classes to the Broadway production, a kind of implicit awareness of Alan Bloom's belief, expressed in *The Closing of the American Mind*, that "deprived of literary guidance, [students] no longer have any image of the perfect soul, and hence do not long to have one...do not even imagine there is such a thing" (Bloom, p. 67). However, the repeated engagements were not undergone with a desire for an encore, for a more intense repetition of a previous response; rather, I began to see new things or old things with new eyes and to discover that I continued to expose myself to a profoundly theological work. As Elizabeth Grossman writes in *Les Miserables: Conversion, Revolution, Redemption*, her little study of the novel:

> Like the sequence of daily biblical readings in a liturgical lectionary, *Les Miserables* aspires to function as a kind of spiritual guide, as a means for reflecting on time and eternity, the secular and the sacred. (Grossman, p. 26)

And Alan Jones notes in *Passion for Pilgrimage* that "*Les Miserables*" is a powerful rendition about the meaning of our longing and a work which "speaks to our ache for reconciliation and resurrection" (Jones, p. 1). Then the idea for this book was born: a theological and spiritual journey through the novel and the musical, treating them as they correspond and as they offer an avenue for spiritual insight to anyone who will risk the pilgrimage. It would also be a way of stating that tears and a standing ovation are not enough, that a real engagement with Hugo and with those who owe a debt to him inhibits anyone from returning to the ordinary business of everyday life. Novel and musical proclaim that life is not "a tale told by an idiot, full of sound and fury, signifying nothing"; rather that life is a new tune that leads one to his true home, that the seemingly "never-ending road to Calvary" is finally the road to glory, rest, peace, and joy.

INTRODUCTION

It is impossible to deny the universal popularity and global success of *"Les Miserables."* The musical has been performed for more than two decades on the London stage and has already been revived on Broadway, albeit for little more than a year. It has also been produced around the world in the language native to the particular country. So well known is the score that one is reminded that such a production is a work of art that exhibits excellence in all areas and that the theater is also a business. Hence, one is subjected at regular intervals to advertisements or even to re-runs on public television of the tenth anniversary special at London's Royal Albert Hall, not merely to signal the ongoing triumph of an epic, but to re-kindle ticket sales as well.

Still trumpeted on television are the enthusiastic, quick, one line responses of theater-goers to the queries of promoters, heard on radio are excerpts from the most popular numbers, and read in newspapers are the reviews of drama critics, most notably when a change in the lead roles has taken place. However, the responses and the excerpts pander to an economic need and betray the power of *"Les Miserables"* to offer an involvement or an engagement which transcends the immediate emotional response while the critic seems more concerned with the technical aspects of production and performance over and against the intellectual and spiritual, and seems to forget that enjoyment is a valid response.

Anthony Tommasini demonstrates such a critical point of view in his *New York Times* article of 20 July 1997. The critic bemoans the loss of the "bracing American musical show" and brands Andrew Lloyd Webber a "British interloper" who "fashion[s] pop riffs, soupy melodies, blatant melodrama, and scenic extravagance." Mr. Tommasini then damns *"Les Miserables"* as "overblown" and sees Hugo's novel as something to be "[slogged] through," a "ponderously historical [book]." Mr. Tommasini contends that such a production, what he defines as the "megamusical," provokes merely an "epic alternative that requires just sitting back, letting it hit you and stilling all mental activity."

It is possible that Victor Hugo, Herbert Kretzmer, Alain Boublil, and Claude-Michel Schonberg never had a predominantly theological or spiritual intent during the composition of the novel or the musical, but for Mr. Tommasini to refer to the book as "ponderous" and the musical as "overblown" misses each. Though I don't believe it to be the case, Hugo's purpose may have been solely to write a novel which indicts those who exploit the wretched and which uses the device of escape and pursuit to hold attention while he advances his cause; the others' intent may have been to create a musical which attempts primarily to capture the essence of its source and, at the same time, produce a memorable and profitable work of art, certainly not to massage the minds of audiences desperate for some sort of relief. In his *New York Post* column of 16 January 2001, I think that Clive Barnes is much closer to the point when he writes that while *"Les Miserables"* is not the greatest musical of all time, it is "superbly efficient [and] while its story may not keep you on the edge of your seat, at least it pins you squarely and firmly to its back." Whatever the intent, the end result is two works which haunt the memory, which refuse to allow us to rest long after we have engaged ourselves with them, and which compel regular re-visits so important are the issues and concepts with which the creators deal. The novel and the musical function in such a way that, when taken together, they allow us to see beyond, even invite us to behold more than is at hand. We cannot manipulate the experience we have, but we can be at the ready, poised, receptive to what is offered.

"*Les Miserables*" does not replace the novel. I don't believe that Kretzmer, Boublil, and Schonberg ever intended it to be a substitute and I think that they would be delighted if their work sent its audience to the original. Like its source, the musical enables us to perceive more clearly the issues we encounter daily: love, hate, mercy, law, wealth, poverty, humility, pride, forgiveness, resentment, life, death, and resurrection. Each work compels us to abandon a casual encounter with existence and look, perceive, and grasp with eyes newly opened the world in which we live; each reminds us that its world is not limited to the nineteenth century, that what transpires in the novel and on the stage is like "looking down the throat of time."

In his work *True Resurrection*, H. A. Williams writes about the "resurrection of the mind," of the need to stock our intellects with what the great writers are saying, of an obligation to become aware that we are Oedipus, Lear, Raskolnikov, and Jean Valjean. In other words, it is not so much that we become aware of the experiences of others, of the various blindnesses, literal and figurative, but that simultaneously we become them, recognize such blindness in ourselves, and say "not 'there but for the grace of God go I,' but 'there I am.'" Williams goes on to remark that when we "meet [such characters] in literature it is ourselves we meet, even if hitherto we have been unaware of our potential for being like that, and however much, once aware of it, it is a case of I dare not waiting upon I would" (*True Resurrection*, p. 89). As a result, *Les Miserables* remains a work which helps us to distill what Alan Ecclestone defines in *Yes To God* as "the truest experience from the events and happenings of our own life" (Ecclestone, p. 58).

Novelist, composer, librettist, all make it a duty to regard *Les Miserables* from the perspective of a poet rather than to complete the novel or leave the theater with the sense of merely having finished something or had a pleasurable experience which is now over, of having, in T. S. Eliot's words, "had the experience but missed the meaning." When Jean Valjean wrestles within his own mind in "A tempest in a human skull," when the chorus advances on the audience in "At the End of the Day," when Javert discovers two ways open before him where before there had been only one, and when the natural and the supernatural combine and time collapses and becomes a present moment at the finale, we engage ourselves, high-lighter in hand, senses tuned, perhaps handkerchief at the ready, in a living response to living works of art. The literary images and metaphors, the light and the dark, the labyrinth of the mind and the labyrinth of the sewers, the musical motifs, and the power of the prose, long lyrical passages on prostitution and the street urchin, prepare us for an encounter with God.

ii

Music provides the underpinning to clarify and strengthen the intense emotions hinted at by Hugo in the one sentence preface to his work where he argues for the enduring relevance of works like *Les Miserables*.

> While through the working of laws and customs there continues to exist a condition of social condemnation which artificially creates a human hell within civilization, and complicates with human fatality a destiny that is divine; while the three great problems of this century, the degradation of man in the proletariat, the subjection of women through hunger, the atrophy of the child by darkness, continue unresolved; while in some regions social asphyxia remains possible; in other words, and in still wider terms, while ignorance and poverty exist on earth, books such as this cannot fail to be of value.

The novel addresses not only all the ills suggested by the clauses which begin with "while," it offers also a solution in the redemptive journey of one man who discovers the nature and power of love and forgiveness. I think that for Hugo what matters most is the substance of Jean Valjean's surrender, the passion which comes to define and direct his life, a passion which participates ultimately in the Passion, the Passion of Christ.

The novel and the musical awaken the one who engages himself with them not only to the moment, but also to an ever-expanding range of experience. In one sense, each art form shapes us and, at the same time, denies that a momentary, superficial, or even cursory response is sufficient, in spite of what critics like Mr. Tommasini suggest. The power of the language and the music, as we shall see, repudiates the merely shallow response, the casual escapist meeting chosen by people like the "I" in Philip Larkin's poem, "A Study of Reading Habits," a short piece which commences with literature being read solely as a means of escape and concludes with the bored exclamation "Get stewed/Books are a load of crap."

The better approach is suggested by the student in the lecture room in Walt Whitman's "When I Heard the Learn'd Astronomer." Here the speaker moves from the illness of the mere acquisition of information to that moment when he abandons the "lecture-room" and "[Looks] up in perfect silence at the stars." He chooses to be bitten by a more encompassing reality, one which cannot be reduced to some sort of utilitarian accumulation of facts. For the careful reader and for the individual on a spiritual journey, it becomes evident that *Les Miserables* renounces the superficial encounter and stimulates instead reason and the imagination, causes us, with Wordsworth, "to see into the life of things."

To read *Les Miserables* interpretively and to surrender to its meaning and power and to see *"Les Miserables"* as an enhancement of the central themes of the novel is to acknowledge that one's life had been impoverished before the meeting. Certainly the same can be said of any masterpiece no matter the discipline. Hence H. A. Williams's remarkable insight in *Becoming What I Am* that perhaps the best prayer we can utter is that of Bartimaeus, "Lord Jesus, let me receive my sight" (Williams, p. 21). The poetic novelist like Hugo and the writers who collaborate on the musical persist at all moments in their attempts to make us see, grasp, perceive. Manipulation there may be in the intricacies of the plot and the causes espoused, but these writers are not manipulative, not attempting to put one over on their audiences. Consequently, novel and musical remain always in a state of being incomplete because we don't finish reading and seeing them; rather, they read and see us and shape us as they do.

To return for a moment to Hugo's prefatory sentence, we notice his perception that some things have gone dead and so he tries to open our eyes to the inherent truths that lie beneath the hell that man has created as he continues to despoil what was once Eden. The power of the novel to transcend narrow confines reminds one of the picture painted by Jonathan Drayton, the artist in Charles Williams's *All Hollow's Eve*, or the encounter between Francis Phelan and Gerald, his dead son, in William Kennedy's *Ironweed*. Drayton's painting of London becomes eventually a picture of London glorified, of the real London beneath and beyond the one in which the artist lives; the journeying Francis, a drunk, engages his past, names his acts, and, in doing so, awakens us to the truth that it is possible to recover a vision of a world which seems empty of awe and wonder, of promise and redemption.

Hugo, Williams, Kennedy, poets and novelists too numerous to mention, all open the eyes of the pilgrim and "free him from the tyranny of the seeming appearance of things". The "while" in Hugo's single sentence preface suggests that the novelist refuses to allow his reader to rest securely in any sort of assumption about human beings as objects to be used or subjugated or destroyed casually as if they were vermin. In this refusal, Hugo joins with (and is joined by) the artist, the musician, and the poet in his attempt to "make all things new." "Behold!" he says and it is a command, an injunction, an imperative, one that must not be ignored.

Hugo wrestles with the whole range of human affairs and searches for ultimate significance in those affairs. The saintly Bishop Myriel, the tormented Javert, the avaricious Thenardier, the idealistic Enjolras, the redeemed Jean Valjean, the suffering Fantine, the young lovers, Marius and Cosette, the unrequited and self-sacrificing Eponine, the homeless urchin Gavroche: all compel a response from the individual on a spiritual journey, from the one who searches for deeper realities which will enflame the soul setting out anew from his departure point or from the one much further along in the spiritual life. Hugo's poetic imagination and Schonberg's rhythmic and thematic repetition weave together a unified experience as the novel illuminates the musical and vice versa.

George Herbert, the seventeenth century priest and poet, called upon God to teach him "in all things thee to see/And what I do in any thing/To do it as for thee" ("The Elixir"). I think that such an invocation is true of Hugo and perhaps of those responsible for the musical as well. Through the imagination, through what C. S. Lewis calls perceptively "the natural organ of meaning," the writers are able to behold and, consequently, to enable us to behold the entrance of the eternal into everything, even if that was not their primary intention or their intention at all. Thus the consequence for the pilgrim on a spiritual journey is the capacity to derive from his engagement the power to live in the presence of God, to draw increasing meaning and depth from the meeting.

William Blake lived "eternity in an hour" and, like Dame Julian who saw God in a hazelnut and Charles Williams's Archdeacon of Fardles, Sybil Conigsby, and Peter Stanhope who see each moment as vertical, as eternally present, rather than as horizontal or chronological, he, as Ecclestone argues, "saw the infinite in the minute particular of every form, knew himself to be the inheritor of all things, and sang with pure joy for his participation in them" (*Yes to God*, p. 61). Similarly, *Les Miserables* is bathed in a light which shines undimmed in the darkness which threatens everywhere and that light is not only a recurring image in the novel but also a dominant motif in the musical where a resurrection to the light shines in the midst of darkness and despair, where we are reminded that the one who journeys in faith need not be overcome by that darkness.

iii

In the second version of the movie "Shadowlands," a young student remarks to C. S. Lewis that his father had told him that "we read in order to know that we are not alone." Hugo's novel and the musical grab the reader and the theater-goer and proclaim to them that they are not alone, that the circumstances of their lives are not isolated no matter how uneventful they may seem. Instead, each circumstance is charged with the Passion and hints at the promise of the resurrection whether the invitation of the charge and the hint are accepted or ignored.

I know people who have found *Les Miserables* to be the darkest of novels, a literal journey into the sewers without the hint of reprieve; I have had students, perhaps much like I was at their age, who viewed the novel only as an exercise in drudgery wondering why they couldn't read the Globe Book, 300 page, large print, complete with pictures edition, if they had to read it at all; I know some men and women who have viewed the musical as three hours of depression deprived of orchestral excellence and without a hint of hope in spite of the final scene. I think that all of these have missed the promise of joy which lies at the heart of the works; I think that they have refused the journey proffered for whatever reason and chosen instead another route or ignored the signposts in the wilderness altogether.

What is necessary is that we must become like Dante and choose to risk the journey when we find ourselves lost in the dark wood with our ways blocked. To embark on the seemingly "never-ending road to Calvary" with Jean Valjean is to choose a course that holds open for us always the infinite possibilities for a new beginning, for a transfiguration that will partake in the Transfiguration.

Kenneth Muir's poem, "*The Transfiguration*," captures this possibility remarkably as a spiritually charged meditation which enables the reader to see with his entire being the way in which Christ's Transfiguration liberates man from the shackles which threaten to imprison him always. The poem does not replace or substitute for the magnitude of the event in the life of Jesus; rather, the poem illuminates the event, envelops it with an even greater majesty, suffuses the reader in a clarity of restored vision. As with the transformation and transfiguration of Jean Valjean, we, too, are "made new to handle holy things," all our seeing is "rinsed and cleansed," and we have returned to us "the clear unfallen world" so that we see Christ present in everything.

The one who chooses to become so engaged discovers what Alan Jones, in *Journey Into Christ,* calls a "voyage to love in the company of love; and the life of love presupposes communion with the loved one" (Jones, p. 22). With Valjean, we become obedient to John Donne's command to tune the instruments of our hearts so that Christ becomes our only music and when that becomes the substance, the goal, the direction of our voyages, we find ourselves in harmony with all creation and, similar to Valjean, we die with "the light upon [our] face[s]," embraced by him who is the Light of the World. Whether that light emanates from the bishop's candlesticks, as it does at the end of the novel, becomes irrelevant.

As in all enduring works of art, Hugo, Kretzmer, Boublil, and Schonberg compel us to catch something of the awe and majesty which lie behind and beyond the mere words and music. They shock us into awareness, into the "Ah ha!" response of experience as we glimpse a reality which transcends the immediate moment and we murmur to ourselves "so this is how things really are." I think that for the Christian pilgrim such a response is even more intense. A. M. Allchin remarks in *The Living Presence of the Past* that this is because, for this pilgrim, "song unites men's minds, making them commune with each other beyond every definition, and unifying them in endless life-giving joy, in a way beyond that which words with their defined and distinct meanings, which divide and limit, are able to do" (Allchin, p. 85).

Allchin goes on to point out that when one chooses to journey into Christ, to participate in the life of God, the myriad riches which result from such a choice are even more "fully expressed in music which overflows through the meanings which the words define" (*Living Presence of the Past*, p. 85). While he certainly had neither Hugo nor the musical in mind, the observation holds true for both as the "infinite riches of meaning" are expressed through diction, imagery, and music. The end result, as suggested earlier, is a poetic language in which multiple layers of meaning are united and in which reader and audience are addressed through their intellects as well as their hearts.

iv

Les Miserables serves an important function in a post-modern world that knows not God or which chooses to reject him. From the opening paragraphs of the novel which introduce us to Bishop Myriel, arguably the catalyst and ultimate focus for all that transpires with regard to Jean Valjean, and the opening notes of the musical which center the audience in the agonizing plight of the chain gang prisoners, *Les Miserables* has the capacity to spark both faith and the imagination, to set them aflame. Reader, listener, audience, individually or collectively, all have the opportunity to respond to the structure and the power of a masterpiece so that they discover, perhaps simultaneously with Jean Valjean, that they are not alone in the universe.

It is as if all are in the process of making the same discovery as did Elwin Ransom, the philologist hero of C. S. Lewis' *Out of the Silent Planet*: that "our mythology is based on a solider reality than we dream: but it is at an almost infinite distance from that base." *Les Miserables* is a work which invokes not only political, social, and moral truths but also deeply spiritual and theological ones to the extent that both novel and musical imitate much larger realities, universal truths about all elements of the human condition. Hugo invites us to journey with Jean Valjean, to see glimpses of reality, and to become artists and poets ourselves as we cooperate with God in his redemption of a fallen world. Even imperfectly we receive intimations and flashes of insight pertaining to reality.

At the end of *"Les Miserables,"* as he prepares to die, Jean Valjean sings "God on high, hear my prayer/Take me now to thy care....Bring me home" and shortly thereafter "forgive me all my trespasses and take me to your glory." Again, like another character in a work by C. S. Lewis, this time Orual, Queen of Glome in *Till We Have Faces*, Valjean discovers that the only answer is God, that all else is but words to be "led out in battle against other words." Hugo and Lewis and other poets and novelists and composers have known all along that art, music, and literature can channel the imagination in such a way that one rises to a level above the verbal and thus is able to grasp reality, perhaps only for a moment at first. We see for an instant all creation transfigured and glory grabs hold of us as we apprehend, as in Edwin Muir's poem, "the one unseeable glory of the everlasting world perpetually at work" (*The Transfiguration*).

Hugo's novel has withstood the test and survived the scrutiny of every type of literary criticism so that it remains a work of genius which continues to fulfill its contention that "[a book] such as this cannot fail to be of value." I believe that the same will be true of the musical each time it is seen and heard and, somewhere in the future, revived. Kretzmer, Boublil, and Schonberg have written a work of art which resonates with life and which, with the novel, helps to lead the Christian pilgrim on his spiritual journey as it transforms and transfigures whatever it touches.

Hugo wrote in the novel that "of all things God has created it is the human heart that sheds the brightest light, and, alas, the blackest despair" (p. 844). His work and the musical based upon it offer hints of the way out of "the dark of ages past," out of the labyrinths and hellish sewers we have created, into a world where "there is a flame that never dies" and "even the darkest night will end and the sun will rise."

The following chapters will attempt to illuminate what the novel and the musical do: invite us by means of theological and spiritual meditations on the characters and experiences as they become ours to begin or continue a journey to the one who is the journey's end. As Grossman notes:

> Imbued with the New Testament notions of grace, charity and self-sacrifice, *Les Miserables* [depicts] the struggle of human conscience with temptation and the eventual

triumph of duty over passion, of freedom over nature. (Grossman, p. 15)

As Hugo does his work, as the composers do theirs, we begin to embrace the world and journey into the freedom that God offers us by attending to the demands made and the joy and glory offered. In the end, what Allchin wrote of T. S. Eliot might be applied easily to *Les Miserables*:

> [Tradition] cannot be inherited, and if you want it you must obtain it by great labour. It involves, in the first place, the historical sense...and the historical sense involves a perception, not only of the pastness of the past, but of its presence, the historical sense compels a man to write not only with his own generation in his bones, but with a feeling that the whole literature of Europe from Homer until today, and within the whole literature of his own country, has a simultaneous existence and compels a simultaneous order. This historical sense which is a sense of the timeless as well as the temporal and of the timeless and the temporal together, is what makes a writer most acutely conscious of his place in time, of his own contemporaneity. (*Living Presence of the Past*, p. 24)

Chapter 1

Sweet Jesus Does Care: The Convict and the Bishop

As the curtain rises on Act I of *"Les Miserables,"* the angry vocal chanting, the repeated sounds of sledges striking rock, and the grunts of prisoners immerse the audience in an arena of pain which pulses like the back and forth motions of a caged animal. If we are attentive, we recognize in the agony of the chain gang a distinctive emptiness, one which is accentuated by two phrases, "You're here until you die" and "You're standing in your grave."

One is exposed immediately to a litany of torture as different members of the tormented group contribute to the chorus of lost hope and unheard prayer. The men are reduced to numbers and, in effect, dehumanized. The sun may be strong, but it brings no light, only sweat and exhaustion in an arid place without refreshment. Correspondingly, in the novel Hugo summarizes the plight of the convict though he speaks explicitly of Jean Valjean.

> Again he felt he had been robbed. Society had robbed him wholesale of a part of his savings; now it was the turn of the individual to rob him in detail. Release, he discovered, was not deliverance. A man may leave prison, but he is still condemned. (p. 104)

The journeys of those in the chain gang appear to have led to Hell without the possibility of redemption. I use the word "appear" because what will transpire with Jean Valjean will affirm Hugo's contention that God has not forsaken the prisoners, that He does care, that while some are quite literally "standing in [their] grave" it is not a grave for the soul.

On the stage, Jean Valjean steps forth from the mass of prisoners, a group so faceless that they are mere grotesques, emblematic of the outcast. In spite of his attempt to recapture his name, "My name is Jean Valjean," he remains just a number to Javert, a cipher defined objectively by his past acts as a thief: "He was released in October 1815, after being imprisoned in 1796 for having broken a window-pane and stolen a loaf of bread" (*Les Miserables*, p. 95). In the musical, the strident tones of Javert intrude on any sense that Valjean might have that he's free.

> *Valjean*: "Yes, that means I'm free."
>
> *Javert*: "No..., you are a thief."
>
> *Valjean*: "I stole a loaf of bread."
>
> *Javert*: "You robbed a house."
>
> *Valjean*: "I broke a window-pane."

The chords struck here reappear throughout the musical whenever the two antagonists face each other and while Jean Valjean will learn to tune his heart to the true source of all music and harmony Javert will remain forever discordant. By identifying these protagonists musically, Kretzmer, Boublil, and Schonberg are following a dramatic tradition set by Wagner in his operas. In the figure of Valjean, there resides an as yet undiscovered and undefined self that will slowly guide his soul toward the true light while in Javert that self is so rigidly understood that it will become impossible for it to be transformed and it will issue in suicide.

For now, Valjean's life has been reduced solely to moments of alienation from society, moments which are made even more terrible when they are accented by his participation in the belief of the prisoners that they have been abandoned by God. Such a perception is made even more emphatic by Javert's eyes, which are those of a judge who distances himself from what is human and regards those before him with disgust, and by his use of a baton across the chest and under the chin of 24601, an image of authoritarian contempt that reviles what it sees before him. While one has not yet been introduced in the musical to the operations of grace, forgiveness, and love, one is aware immediately of the power of such misdirected passion, such intense commitment to the letter of the law which merely counts offenses and starves, scorches, and scars the miscreants emotionally, physically, and psychologically until they "learn the meaning of the law."

Such experiences impress themselves indelibly on the mind of the individual, so much so that in the case of Valjean his memory of them is awakened. The first occasion takes place in the convent during those times when he would let his "thoughts drift in meditation."

> He would recall the wretchedness of his former companions.... They lived without names, were known only by numbers and to some extent turned into numbers themselves, eyes and voices lowered, hair cropped, subject to the law and to constant humiliation." (p. 488)

Later, when he and Cosette see a chain gang, he beholds what his life was like before he began his journey to salvation: an existence which seeps into the life of the convict like a cancer making its way stealthily through his soul until he becomes a pariah dehumanized by society. In response to Cosette's questions, "Father, what are these men?" and "Are they still human?" he can reply "Felons" and "sometimes" (p. 786). Valjean cannot forget the faces of misery to be seen in such a gathering, faces which bear "the stamp of ignominy" (p. 784) As Javert has used his baton on Valjean, a guard uses the end of his club as if "to plunge it into the heart of human garbage" (p. 785).

Such memory is seared into the psyche of the individual so that his eyes will be "eyes no longer," but "fathomless mirrors" which "no longer see reality but reflect the memory of past events" (p. 785); such memory can be alleviated only by acts of love, in Valjean's case by "two of God's houses [that] had taken him in" (p. 493). The process of redemption is begun and continued by the bishop and those in the convent (p. 488) so that the end result is a "heart melted in gratitude" and a love that is "magnified" (p. 491). It is agonizingly difficult to face a "world that always hates," to live in tension as the drama of one's life is played out on an unfamiliar stage, but Valjean bears witness to the actuality that such choices are made and he comes to discover on his journey to Calvary that the world hated Christ before it ever hated him.

Tension reigns in the confrontation between Valjean and Javert, a tension which always simmers and threatens to boil over in all subsequent encounters and which must exist wherever men who seek to be free are reduced to slaves and defined by numbers. Yet horrible as this confrontation is, it marks a first step not only on Valjean's journey toward Calvary and the City of God, but also toward an awareness of the power of conscience, a recognition that will continue to emerge and develop; in another sense, it is a first step on a journey into meaning in the midst of the threat of meaninglessness.

Hugo iterates often his belief that darkness and hatred threaten to consume the world, a threat not confined to the nineteenth century; he also believes that small affirmations can arise from within such danger, that light can shine out of the darkness and stench of chain gangs and sewers. Someone like Jean Valjean may be battered by systematic forces which he cannot grasp, yet the chance encounter with one who sees with eyes of love, like Bishop Myriel, offers an opportunity for engagement in a different realm. Even when the brutality of a legal system and the horror of a chain gang etch themselves into the psyche of an individual so that, as Grossman notes, he "wears his prison brand both inside and outside" (p. 63), the light of love is not totally eclipsed.

Without the intervention of the bishop, an intervention not adequately prepared for in the musical because an examination of the bishop's life would function as a digression, one could not blame an audience for concluding early on that the Chorus is correct, that "Sweet Jesus doesn't care." One might draw easily the inference that estrangement does lead to final separation and that everything which defines one's life can be extinguished.

However, Valjean's meeting with Myriel begins to produce a different response, one which hints at hope and which has its roots in the love of God. The encounter between the two men acts as the catalyst for the initial steps in what is to become an ongoing experience of resurrection. It is the kind of encounter which serves as a paradigm for all those acts of charity which spring from the gospel and which raise lost and wandering souls, withered nearly to the point of non-existence, as good as dead, to a moment of hope. In this sense, the novel and the musical explore a common theme: that Jean Valjean or any other man, no matter how brutal, violent, and vindictive he once was (much more apparent in the novel than on the stage), can be raised from his own dead past. This is not mere melodrama but Hugo's response to that society which threatens to brand the sinner to the extent that he cries out "I'm not even a dog!" (p. 79)

The frightened and self-righteous deny shelter to such a man and his number and yellow ticket become "the mark of Cain" so that all doors are locked to him. In the novel, Hugo pauses to reflect for a moment on such a plight.

> Can human nature ever be wholly and radically transformed? Can the man whom God has made good be made wicked by man? Can the soul be shaped in its entirety by destiny and made evil because destiny is evil?...Is there not in every human soul, and was there not in the soul of Jean Valjean, an essential spark, an element of the divine, indestructible in this world and immortal in the next, which goodness can perceive, nourish, and fan into a glorious flame, and which evil can never quite extinguish? (p. 98)

Hugo answers these questions, especially the last, throughout the novel and in doing so maintains that one's soul cannot be blotted out. Though his freedom is balanced against his imprisonment, though he sings in the musical "Never forget the years, the waste. Never forgive them for what they've done," a spark of love, compassion, and forgiveness remains alive in Valjean which is perceived only by the bishop, a spark which will redeem that inward despair which contrasts with "freedom is mine," a spark which will come to know even Javert as a living presence who cannot be reduced merely to a word (enemy), and thus a spark which enlarges Valjean's identity rather than shrinks it, a spark which overcomes the fear and anger which threaten to continue to imprison Valjean even after he is released from prison.

As Jean Valjean searches for work and shelter, the prose and the music echo the anger of the prison chant and he is observed "with a vague misgiving" since "it would have been hard to find a traveler of more disreputable aspect" (p. 71), a man who elicits only "excited and hostile looks," and is rejected by "those honest men like me" whom we discover are far from honest. Their hatred is imbedded deeply within them and camouflages itself in their righteous response to Valjean's earlier musing "And now let's see what this new world will do for me!"– a musing that is plaintive, tinged with hope and despair.

We are reminded immediately in the musical (but only after being introduced to Bishop Myriel in the novel) of the lethal nature of such rejection and of how such poison works quickly to embitter its victim. The clear taste of freedom is contaminated by the acrimony of rejection. However, such loss of hope is not the last word. This novel and this musical are about a fact: that no matter how lost, how desperate, or how rejected a man may be, God never abandons him, never leaves him desolate. Valjean's journey confirms this and it is the Bishop of Digne, the "old fool [who trusts Valjean]" and is wise beyond Valjean's knowing, who mediates God's love.

The kindly Bishop of Digne occupies only a few moments on stage in the production of "*Les Miserables.*" Most likely he will be remembered for several memorable statements he makes to Jean Valjean: "And remember this, my brother; see in this some higher plan. You must use this precious silver to become an honest man. By the witness of the martyrs, by the Passion and the Blood, God has raised you out of darkness; I have bought your soul for God."

These statements mark a seminal moment in the play, one which imposes itself positively on Jean Valjean's memory and conscience throughout the rest of the musical, but they are easily passed over by the careless listener, by someone unfamiliar with the novel, and it is just as easy to ignore the evidence which defines the bishop as the catalyst, even the focal point, for everything that Valjean will do. However, it is in the novel alone that one discovers the reasons for the bishop's statements and for his central role in Jean Valjean's life. Hugo articulates precisely his justification for the essential and successful role the bishop plays when he writes that "he had his own way of looking at things. I think he derived it from the Gospel."

In essence, then, the statements cited from the musical and the accompanying acts which define his life do not occur in a vacuum or at a moment; they find their roots in the depth of one's relationship with God from whom all goodness flows. That such a relationship has the power to re-define one's life is evident from the first page of the novel where Charles Myriel, widowed, undergoes a re-birth of immense proportions.

> Amid the distractions and frivolities that occupied his life, did it happen that he was suddenly overtaken by one of those mysterious and awful repulsions which, striking at the heart, change the nature of a man who cannot be broken by outward disasters affecting his life and fortune? (p. 19)

The obvious answer to the question is "yes." The supernatural has impinged on his life in such a way that, while "no one can say" exactly what has transpired, he becomes a priest. The consequence is that his life is re-shaped and this conversion prepares him for all his future acts of kindness and love. The ultimate reality of God becomes an objective fact which makes possible all his moral acts.

The Bishop of Digne dominates the first one hundred pages of the novel and it is through him that we develop an awareness of what happens to an individual engaged in the discovery that he shares in the betrayal of Christ, that such a betrayal is not limited to the act of Judas. Out of that discovery arises the power of the Cross to raise hope and trust for those like Jean Valjean who have become outcasts and believe that hope is no longer possible for them. Because of this discovery, Myriel is able to commit to an act of faith, what Alan Ecclestone calls an authentic "yes" to God. Thus the bishop becomes a source of light in the midst of darkness, the catalyst for Valjean's redemption, for the spiritual and moral growth which enables the ex-convict to overcome his debilitating anger. As he will raise Jean Valjean to the light, he will be a constant source of illumination rather than just an occasional flicker, and he will enable Valjean to raise first Fantine and then Cosette to him who is the "Light of the world."

It is important to realize that Bishop Myriel never loses his humility, that he never succumbs to any temptation to see himself as the light of the world. Such a choice places him in a position antagonistic to other potentates in the church, "the fashionable bishops, well-endowed and urbane dignitaries, on excellent terms with the world" (p. 63). These men of power in the church seek their own light whereas Myriel is content to be a vessel by which others, especially Valjean, will see everything else.

Kenneth Leech notes in *True Prayer* that "orthodoxy is about being consumed by glory: the word means right glory. To be orthodox is to be set alight by the fire of God" (Leech, p. 63). Such is the orthodoxy of Monseigneur Bienvenu, "humble, penurious, and retiring" (p. 63), who chooses a life so different from that of other bishops that other young priests, seeking advancement or preferment, go elsewhere. His orthodoxy is not that of creeds and canons, though he believes in and adheres to them; rather, it is an orthodoxy of love and compassion manifested in all his acts.

Myriel's theology is defined by personal involvement rather than mere political assent and the end result is a depth of engagement which affects the lives of others, notably the women who live with him as well as Jean Valjean. Such a theological stance is summarized accurately by William Law.

All outward power that we exercise in the things about us is but a shadow in comparison of that inward power that resides in our will, imagination, and desire; these communicate with eternity and kindle a life which always reaches either Heaven or hell. (cited in Hadfield, p. 94)

And again by Daniel Halevy.

"The Christian follows a master who bore a heavy burden; he has no ambition for the vain exercise of power and temporal excellence; he is the burden-bearer of creation."

(cited in *Yes to God*, p. 7)

So unlike his ecclesiastical brethren, the orbit of selfishness is not one in which Myriel moves. Thus he develops a selflessness out of which arises a quiet and genuine joy which has the power to convict Jean Valjean, a selflessness which illustrates what is implied by the petition in the Prayer Book Collect for the fourth Sunday in Advent: that, at his coming, Christ "may find in us a mansion prepared for himself." Early in the novel, the bishop exchanges his episcopal residence for the building that has served as a hospital so that "twenty-six paupers [are] moved into the palace and the bishop [takes] up residence in the hospital" (p. 22). As Herbert O'Driscoll notes in his meditation on the Collect in *Prayers for the Breaking of Bread*, the bishop builds a place for his soul to live in. The mansion which Myriel prepares awaits a guest and the guest is God; he prepares the house of the self for the presence of God (p. 11).

The simplicity and humility of the bishop are always in the forefront, a never-ending lesson on the pattern of existence to be lived by those who have engaged themselves with God. The contrast with the potentates is sharp and Hugo reminds us that such an exercise incurs displeasure.

Among his disconcerting utterances was one that he let fall one evening in the home of one of his most eminent colleagues: "So many handsome clocks and carpets! So many rich liveries! It must be very embarrassing. I would not care to live with all this luxury reminding me that there are people who are cold and hungry. There are the poor! There are the poor!" (pp. 59-60)

Myriel refuses to surrender to the lure of the temporal at the expense of the eternal. He repudiates clerical wealth and adopts mercy instead because he believes that this is what the gospel has shown him. His focus is on the inner growth of the soul, on the exercise of charity as opposed to the exercise of the acquisition of the merely material and the embrace of political power in the realm of the holy. Though he admits willingly that he "should find it hard to give up eating with silver" (p. 38) and though he treasures the candlesticks inherited from a great aunt, he is able to enjoy these things but not as possession. He is never in danger of having the objects possess him and so when the moment arrives he is able to relinquish them.

The possessive "mine" which devours such figures as Tolkien's Gollum and Conrad's Nostromo and the young revelers in *The Pardoner's Tale* has no hold over the bishop. That is because the bishop has embraced a true poverty, a refusal to be bitten by the itch to own, especially at the expense of the poor. He illustrates well Hugo's contention that the "first proof of charity in a priest, above all in a bishop, is poverty" (p. 60). He even repents having kept the silver which he enjoys for so long and thus, when it is returned to him by the constables who have apprehended Jean Valjean, he is able to give it away to Valjean along with the candlesticks.

"So here you are! He cried to Valjean. "I'm delighted to see you. Had you forgotten that I gave you the candlesticks as well? They're silver like the rest, and worth a good two hundred francs. Did you forget to take them?" (*Les Miserables*, pp. 110-111)

And from the musical:

Constable: You maintain he made a present of this silver.

Bishop: That is right. But my friend, you left so early surely something slipped your mind. You forgot I gave these also— would you leave the best behind?

Because of the depth of what took place before his return from Italy, because of the authentic nature of his response to God occasioned by that event, Bishop Myriel continues to affirm his initial response in the present.

Since all life for him is an extension of the creative activity of God, of the Incarnation and Passion of Christ, he is able to see into the heart of Jean Valjean and perceive there that virtue which all others have believed to be beyond reach. For him, the Gospel brings the recognition that people are more than just people, that all are worthy of love. He does not merely appeal to others to help the poor, to consider their suffering; he does so himself. Jesus' command, "Love one another as I have loved you," defines his existence.

> "To him everything was contained in those words, his whole doctrine, and he asked no more." (p. 69)

This creed which functions as the theological cornerstone of the bishop's life and which is assumed to be folly by a senator, an acquaintance of the bishop's who fancies himself a philosopher and who prefers the perspective that men are at war with each other and "victory to the strongest" (p. 69), bears fruit in the life of Jean Valjean and substantiates the theological belief that love, joy, and peace have their source in God. To paraphrase Alan Ecclestone, but with regard to Charles Myriel, "the Yes pronounced in human history by [the bishop] who has endeavored so to shape his life as to conform as truly as he could to that pattern Christ had set" enables others to pronounce their Yes as well (*Yes to God*, p. 2).

So shaped and directed by the principle of life has the bishop's life become that when money is donated for a new altar, he gives it to the poor: "the soul of an unfortunate who thanks God for consolation is the best of altars" (p. 41). And later he remarks to the two women that "we must never fear robbers or murderers.... What we have to beware of is the threat to our souls" (p. 42).

Hugo summarizes the bishop's saintly existence in the following passage:

The days of his life, as we have seen, were filled with prayer, with the celebration of the offices, the giving of alms, the consoling of the afflicted, the tilling of his garden plot; with brotherliness, frugality, hospitality, renunciation, trust, study, and toil. Filled, indeed, is the correct word, for the bishop's days overflowed with goodness of thought and word and action....

He pondered on the greatness and the living presence of God, on the mystery of eternity in the future and, even more strange, eternity in the past, on all the infinity manifest to his eyes and to his senses; and without seeking to comprehend the incomprehensible he contemplated these things. (p. 67)

It is the essence of the bishop's life, and subsequently of Valjean's, to be about the "business of heaven," to counter the agony and despair which permeates any society at any point in history with the reality of hope. He can do this because his experience has corroborated his faith, because for him "no problem of faith was ever hypocritically resolved" (p. 65).

What this chapter has done is look at the life of Charles Myriel, a character based on a real person, an actual figure who befriended a released convict. The love of the saintly bishop has the power to bind together generations which extend far into the future. Because he centers his life on God and because his holiness issues from that focus, he is able to perceive in the outcast who comes to his door a dimension that is imperceptible to someone like Javert and those who have turned him away. He embraces the essence of that prayer attributed to King Alfred: "To see Thee is the end and the beginning. Thou carriest me and Thou goest before. Thou art the journey and the journey's end." As he gives freely to Valjean, so Valjean gives of himself to others—to the poor, to Fantine and Cosette, even to his enemies, at first Fauchelevant and then Javert. As the bishop sees clearly, he enables others to see as well; he perceives that goodness which derives from God and which is part of creation and which many have ceased to perceive at all. The series of responses which he makes are the kind which, argues Hugo, all desire to make.

The gift of the silver is an act which, as Ecclestone points out, is itself "a pledge or wagering of some thing or person, the mortgaging of life itself, the bet of faith" (*Yes to God*, p. 9). The Bishop of Digne has navigated his journey to freedom and the City of God by the light of Christ, by that light which is discovered in the breaking of bread and the pouring of wine, in the outcast figure of Jean Valjean.

Chapter 2

I Have Bought Your Soul for God:
The First Step on the Journey Home

In *Grace and Glory*, E. L. Mascall writes that "grace is nothing other than the beginning of glory in us." Such a definition clarifies the awe present when Jean Valjean first encounters the Bishop of Digne. Charles Myriel exudes an aura of holiness and humility, an aura which proclaims that this silver-haired man dressed in white has caught the glory of the God whom he has chosen to embrace and, as such, radiates glory to others. That is the power of grace, the unmerited and yet free gift of God to all who choose to receive it. Invited into a relationship and having accepted the invitation, having been himself transformed and transfigured, Charles Myriel now gives freely to others what he has received from God.

It is not merely some sort of transaction between creditor and debtor but a joyous return based on an intimate apprehension of what God has done for him. Consequently, as is even more evident in the novel, the bishop acts selflessly and without judgment; the recipient of God's free gift of grace, he becomes the mediator of that same grace to Valjean, without conditions attached.

> "You need have told nothing. This house is not mine but Christ's. It does not ask a man his name but whether he is in need. You are in trouble, you are hungry and thirsty, and so you are welcome. You need not thank me for receiving you in my house. No one is at home here except those seeking shelter. Let me assure you, passer-by though you are, that

this is more your home than mine. Everything in it is yours. Why should I ask your name? In any case, I knew it before you told me."

The man looked up with startled eyes. "You know my name?"

"Of course," said the bishop. "Your name is brother." (p. 87)

Valjean, denied room at other inns, is welcomed by the bishop and one is reminded that to make room in one's life for the stranger and the outcast is pure gift. For there to be no room for Valjean elsewhere is to suggest that it is not mere space that is lacking, but also the absence of room in the hearts and minds of those who reject him. Because, as David Adam points out in *Border Lands*, the bishop opens his residence to another, thereby opening himself to the Other who is such an integral part of his life (Adam, p. 43). Another place is set for the meal, clean sheets are placed on the bed, and the dinner is served—a watery broth, bread, figs, cheese, and a bottle of old wine—a meal which is symbolically Eucharistic. The meal provides the first step in the nourishment of Jean Valjean's body and soul for the journey home.

The principle of hospitality to one's brother is illustrated in a story which Alan Jones recounts in *Passion for Pilgrimage*. A rabbi asks his students about the dawning of true light: "When can you tell that the day is breaking?" Several answers are given which rely on the ability to see things with the eyes rather than with the inner heart. After several less than satisfactory responses from his students, the rabbi responds to their demand for an answer so frustrated are they in their own attempts. He counters, "Day breaks when you look at a man or a woman and know that he or she is your brother or your sister. Until you can do that, no matter what time of day it is, it is always night" (*Passion for Pilgrimage*, p. 63). This paradigm is similar to Saint-Exupery's contention in *The Little Prince* "That it is only with the heart that one sees rightly; what is essential is invisible to the eye."

One cannot overestimate the efficacy of a Eucharistic meal, even if it exists in microcosm, a service in miniature, most likely marked formally only by grace yet nevertheless accented with hospitality and generosity. Though absent from the musical, this efficacy becomes apparent in the novel when Jean Valjean, having awakened at two o'clock in the morning, obsessed by the silver, contemplates the murder of the bishop. However, the bread and wine of the simple dinner exert a different power than anticipated, a power foreshadowed in the bishop's words from the musical.

> There is wine here to revive you. There is bread to make you strong. There's a bed to rest 'till morning. Rest from pain and rest from wrong.

The repetition of "rest" suggests more than mere physical respite. Present also is the sense of refreshment for the moral and spiritual life of the outcast. The agony of rejection and the desire for revenge are set aside and replaced by tranquility. As Valjean hovers over the bishop's bed and an almost miraculous light surrounds Myriel, a moonlight which shines where clouds have been torn asunder "as though by a deliberate act" and which falls on the bishop's face, he encounters here "serenity, hope, beatitude, something more than a smile and little short of radiance, the reflection of light that was not to be seen" (p. 108). He beholds something which he can neither define nor comprehend at the moment, but, as C. S. Lewis suggests somewhere, the flag of truth and love, compassion and mercy, has been planted "within the fortress of a rebel soul." This contrast is even more marked when one begins to have those faint stirrings from deep within prompted by a knowledge of the void and meaninglessness he has endured which is now measured against the love and compassion generated by an awareness that nothing earthly can satisfy what one desires.

For the Bishop of Digne, the symbols of "broken bread and wine outpoured [are] sufficient food for the journey" (*Journey Into Christ*, p. 51). It is easy to infer that for him every meal is a celebration of the Eucharist and thus bread and wine are able to work in him at the supernatural level. As these two essential elements nourish the bishop's soul, they bring into Valjean's presence all the goodness of love and labor that can be mustered. As William Temple notes in his commentary on John's Gospel, bread and wine "are the gift of God rendered serviceable by the labor of man" (p. 81) so that the bread and old wine which have been given to Valjean begin to transmit to his soul a "satisfaction that endures eternally" (p. 87). At the supernatural level, bread and wine function always as a symbol of love, a love that is magnified and deepened as it is broken and given away. What the bishop has learned and gathered to himself, he now practices.

Of course, Valjean does not yet comprehend this in such terms as expressed above and the bishop never plays the part of the learned theologian by offering an explanation. However, that is no matter; the truth exists and operates even when not articulated explicitly. The bishop has long ago discovered that to drink of the cup is to engage in the pain, to become part of the story of Christ even at those moments early in his life when that story had not yet been fully discovered nor understood. The dynamic nature of the efficacy of the Eucharistic meal is best expressed by Temple when he comments on the sixth chapter of John's Gospel and notes that when Jesus refers to himself as the Bread of Life the negatives in "'never hunger...never thirst' are the strongest in the Greek language. Hunger and thirst become simply impossible to the one who comes" (p. 87), as the bishop has and Jean Valjean will. Similarly, Ephrem the Syrian writes that "In the Bread we eat the power that cannot be eaten; in the Wine we drink the Fire that cannot be drunk." And from "Christmas," a poem by John Betjeman:

> No love that in a family dwells,
> No carolling in frosty air,
> Nor all the steeple-shaking bells
> Can with this single truth compare—
> That God was man in Palestine
> And lives today in Bread and Wine.

> (Cited in *True Prayer*)

As the bishop has drunk deeply of the cup and eaten the bread of life, he has come to share in the life of Christ. At the same time, he extends that life to Valjean in such a way that the icy bitterness which exists within Valjean begins to thaw and he is provided with a different kind of food which will sustain him on his journey.

God will become the focal point of Valjean's life, even when his love for Cosette threatens that relationship. This is expressed most forcefully in his presence at the barricade, in "Bring Him Home" and its reprise at the end of the musical, and in his confession to Marius, and that focus is apparent even when Jean Valjean is unaware of it. Valjean has received a gift from God in the goodness of the bishop and that gift, manifested in the lodging, the meal, the silver, and the calling of Valjean by the name of "brother," commences his transformation as he begins to participate in the life and nature of God. The strange, poor, weary convict has been welcomed into the Eucharistic banquet and has been revived by the wine and strengthened by the bread to the point that he decides not to murder the bishop. This would seem sufficient, but there is more as the bishop enters into a bargain with Valjean of which Valjean is unaware.

The nature of the bargain is made evident through a series of imperatives in the novel and the musical.

The bishop came up to him and said in a low voice:

> "Do not forget, do not ever forget, that you have promised me to use the money to make yourself an honest man."

Valjean, who did not recall having made any promise, was silent. The bishop had spoken the words shortly and deliberately. He concluded with a solemn emphasis:

> "Jean Valjean, my brother, you no longer belong to what is evil but to what is good. I have bought your soul to save it from black thoughts and the spirit of perdition, and I give it to God."

(p. 111)

An almost exact paraphrase occurs in the musical. The harsh, worldly, staccato accusations of the soldier are contrasted with the bishop's lyrical legato melody expressing his love and compassion. The notes of the final "bargain" are placed in a somber, low register reinforcing their gravity.

> But remember this, my brother:
> See in this some higher plan.
> You must use this precious silver
> To become an honest man.
> By the witness of the martyrs,
> By the Passion and the Blood,
> God has raised you out of darkness
> I have bought your soul for God!

Such an act on the part of Bishop Myriel expresses to Jean Valjean that another world exists outside of the one defined by the harshness of chain gangs and rejection, that resurrection is a present reality, undergone at all moments, not an event confined to some moment after death. The world perceived by Jean Valjean is transitory when contrasted with the solidity of that world inaugurated by God.

When the bishop invokes the "witness of the martyrs" and the "Passion and the Blood," he invokes history, the living and the dead, the Cross which, in T. S. Eliot's words, is at the "still point of the turning world." The "witness," the "Passion," and the "Blood" (note the capitals) are gifts which cut across the boundaries of linear time. And when the bishop adds "I have bought your soul for God," he inverts the bargain made by Faust with, as Grossman points out, Satan (p. 29) and announces that the ultimate purpose of any such gift is the recipient's salvation. It is God who raises Jean Valjean "out of darkness" and, observes Grossman, "the mental and emotional chains that [have kept] the former galley slave shackled to his past [are] broken" (p. 29). The bishop becomes the catalyst for a kind of volcanic eruption as contradictory feelings explode within Valjean as he plays out the drama of the moment, feelings which Alan Jones characterizes as "the longing, the gratitude, the disappointment, the aching, the anger" (*Passion for Pilgrimage*, p.

82). The immensity of such an act is best expressed by Allchin in *Living Presence of the Past* .

> ...from my own personal hell of despondency and self-destruction, of paralyzing guilt and anxiety, from a strait-jacket of circumstances not of my own devising, I myself am lifted up, restored to true relationship, by him who descended into death to find me. (p. 120)

As with the "I" in George Herbert's "Redemption," Valjean discovers salvation where he least expects it, not among "theeves (sic) and murderers" as in the poem, though that, too, is possible, but in an episcopal gift which is itself an invitation to discover a new identity, a new way of coming to grips with the world and with others so that as he ventures on the "never-ending road to Calvary" he will live and not die. As Grossman points out so lucidly, "his conversion thus begins as a transformation of perspective when he apprehends the peculiar logic of love and forgiveness" (p. 29). Such a discovery is made not only in a single moment by one individual but by many individuals at every moment in history. Someone beholds the face of God in another and begins to live.

Jean Valjean has been consecrated for a journey and his response is a leap of faith, one which can initiate reader and audience into a new realm of love, wonder, and awe. Herbert wrote in "The Elixir" that

> A man that looks on glasse
> On it may stay his eye;
> Or if he pleaseth, through it passe,
> And then the heav'n espie.

Such sight has been developed by the bishop to the extent that his faith, love, and imagination cooperate with his reason, rather than at the expense of it, to perceive what is holy in Valjean. But it is not just an inherent holiness; it is also an incompleteness. The bishop recognizes that to be thus unfinished is part of what Alan Jones defines as one's glory and pain. Glory because Myriel knows that there is always more to be revealed as Valjean advances from "glory to glory"; pain because being unfinished reminds one at all times that his destiny lies elsewhere. Hugo awakens us so that we see, as Ecclestone argues in *Yes to God,* all things in light of their eternal reality (p. 63).

In the gospel story, Jesus looks on a rich young man and loves him. Following his master, the bishop does the same to Jean Valjean. He sees all that lies within and calls him "brother" and thus he functions not only as someone wooing the sinner to the glory that has been promised but also as the individual who hurls a challenge at the outcast to discover the ultimate reality which is God himself. The voyage which now unfolds is a liberation from darkness and despair; it is a resurrection story; it is a journey to freedom and a refusal to be shackled by the bitterness of revenge and the smothering, choking anger which threatens to suffocate existence; it is to say No to the darkness and the chaos which threaten and to embrace the light instead.

Having been rescued by the bishop's lie and having entered into a mysterious bargain which he cannot recall, Jean Valjean undertakes a journey to freedom, a pilgrimage compelled by the generosity, kindness, and compassion of the bishop. During the course of this journey, which will last his life, his encounters will unveil slowly to him that he need never renounce Jean Valjean, that God will use his light and darkness in order to liberate him. As he nearly shrieks "What have I done? Sweet Jesus, what have I done?" he begins to grope toward what Ecclestone so profoundly articulates as "that which alone can satisfy the profoundest need of our human life: to know that we are known and loved by God" (p. 7). The Jesus of the chain gang chorus, the Jesus who seems not to care, is now implored to provide the answer and the fact of the story is that He does. The Valjean of the beginning, the Valjean whose eyes are blind or distorted so that he cannot see clearly the light that is before him, has now had the bishop begin to open his eyes to the reality of existence so that his journey will be a process of discovering how to see.

The transforming love of Charles Myriel is the catalytic element in Valjean's journey, the encounter which renders meaningful all his other acts. The bishop's knowledge that God loves him, that his own love for Valjean is his free response to the knowledge that he is known and loved by God, is transmitted to Valjean who will spend the rest of his life learning to grasp the powerful implications of such knowledge and then communicate that knowledge to others. As Valjean reflects on the incredible fact that the bishop has called him "brother," he discovers that his soul has been touched, that he has been taught love, and that questions have now been raised about existence in a world that the bishop has turned upside down. Valjean can escape from the "whirlpool of sin" in which he finds himself as he learns to name his past, see the shadows for what they are, and choose to be himself raised to the splendor of the light. The labyrinth of his existence has now been provided with a way out so that his decision to trust the bishop is the first step in his placing of his hand in the hand of the One who will enable him to find his way home, as Jones suggests in *Passion for Pilgrimage* (p. 85).

In the musical, Valjean asks a series of questions of himself and these provide a glimpse into his inner landscape at this moment in time: "What have I done?" is repeated; "Have I fallen so far?"; "Yet why did I allow this man to touch my soul and teach me love?"; "Can such things be?"; "What spirit comes to move my life?"; "Is there another way to go?" Each question echoes in its own way Ivan Ilych's thrice repeated question in Tolstoy's *The Death of Ivan Ilych*: "What if my life has really been wrong?" That such characters can even ask such questions suggests the numbing conflict which exists within and the simultaneous beginning of recognition. Add to this the musical shift in *"Les Miserables,"* which begins with "Yet why did I...," and one perceives the stunning contrast which exists between love and hatred. Valjean arrives at the bishop's in one frame of mind and departs in the realization that somehow, mysteriously, only under the operation of divine grace, God loves him as unlovely as he is.

As Ecclestone asserts at several points in *Yes To God*, such a moment of discovery and perception is fraught with immense opportunities for choice: it either arrests us on our journey, or turns us back, or bows us to the earth (p. 42). In other words, maintains Ecclestone, we see and shudder or we see and exult. The answer to the prayer of Bartimaeus, "let me receive my sight," changes the course of one's life so that Jean Valjean, trying his own case (*Les Miserables*, pp. 96-98), begins to redefine the path his life will take. Though he cannot yet fathom the love and generosity of the bishop ("He was overwhelmed by new and strange sensations, among them a kind of anger, he did not know against whom" [*Les Miserables*, p. 112]), he chooses to respond, to refuse to be inert or unmoved, and thus he chooses to risk because he commits himself to acts which are matters of eternity.

The kindness of the bishop knocks Valjean off his feet, so violently that "nothing remains but the cry of [his] hate," a cry that will dissolve as he discovers that such love can be. The security of righteous anger and the embracing of vengeance now must begin to be abandoned. The reality of a divine power that touches the soul and teaches love bears directly on the recipient so that Valjean finds himself at a moment of decision, a moment which demands choice and which compels the implicit realization, imaged by C.S. Lewis in *The Great Divorce*, that all roads are not "radii of a circle and where all, if followed long enough, will therefore draw gradually nearer and finally meet at the centre" (pp. v-vi). As in the bishop's own life, as with any other man, Valjean will discover that freedom can be gained only by obedience to that command which has shaped the life of the bishop and comes from Christ – "Love one another as I have loved you." Such obedience is freely chosen, of one's own accord, because it issues from the joyful recognition that one knows he is loved.

The discovery is not just for an instant; rather Valjean continues to be taught by God because, in the metaphor of the classroom, all the subject matter is never fully covered. Life becomes a school of prayer. The bishop's instruction is not the end and the escape which Valjean makes is not just from the shackles of the prison but also into an increased sense of his past, an awareness which makes him more conscious of the present, of his own time and place. It is Hugo's way of pointing out to the reader that the past is contemporary with us, that the past "is known as involving the timeless as well as the temporal." When the librettist has Valjean sing "Take an eye for an eye....He told me that I had a soul," it is as if Valjean understood paradox, grasped that the past is present and impinges on us directly. As Allchin notes, "it is as we are truly able to recollect and remember it that we become able to live fully in the present, creatively toward the future" (*Living Presence of the Past*, p. 94).

The ensuing encounter with Petit-Gervais, an encounter omitted in the musical, during which Valjean steals the boy's forty-sou piece, stresses the battle which rages within Valjean's soul, a battle which anticipates the later chapter, "A tempest in a human skull." Yet the writers of the musical capture the essential conflict inherent in the meeting as Valjean begins his search for the boy in order to undo the theft. However, he is unable to restore the money and the battle is joined: "a momentous and decisive battle between the evil in himself and the goodness in that other man" (p. 116). Valjean is as wretched as anyone in the throes of conscience – "Je suis un miserables" – and arrives at what Grossman expresses as a "moment of self-awareness that expresses his sense of both wretchedness and villainy" (p. 30).

However, such awareness can lead to a positive action, not just to despair, and later on in the chapter alluded to above we discover that Valjean has undergone a transfiguration: "...following his encounter with the boy, Petit-Gervais. Thereafter, as we have seen, he was a changed man, enacting in his life what the bishop had sought to make of him. It was more than a transformation; it was a transfiguration" (p. 208). The Transfiguration on Mount Tabor transfigures Valjean, indeed, all of creation, and he will learn to see Fantine, the poor, Cosette, Marius, perhaps Javert above all, in the light of Christ's transfigured glory. As the poet wrote, it is to "cut the tree in half and I am there." The magnitude of Valjean's transfiguration is of such importance that the passage which expresses Hugo's omniscient insight must be cited in its entirety.

It was one of those moments of blinding yet frighteningly calm insight when the thought goes so deep that it passes beyond reality. The tangible world is no longer seen; all that we see, as though from outside, is the world of our own spirit.

Thus he contemplated himself, as it were face to face, and there arose in his vision, at some mysterious depth, a sort of light resembling that of a torch. But as he looked more closely at this light growing in his consciousness he saw that it had a human form and that it was the bishop.

His mind's eye considered these two men now presented to him, the bishop and Jean Valjean. Only the first could have overshadowed the second. By a singular process special to this kind of ecstasy, as his trance continued the bishop grew and gained splendour in his eyes, while Jean Valjean shrunk and faded. A moment came when Valjean was no more than a shadow, and then he vanished entirely. The bishop alone remained, flooding that unhappy soul with radiance.

Jean Valjean wept for a long time, sobbing convulsively with more than a woman's abandon, more than the anguish of a child. And as he wept a new day dawned in his spirit, a day both wonderful and terrible. He saw all things with a clarity that he had never known before—his past life, his first offense and long expiation, his outward coarsening and inward hardening, his release enriched with so many plans for revenge, the incident at the bishop's house, and this last abominable act, the robbing of a child, rendered more shameful by the fact that it followed the bishop's forgiveness. He saw all this, the picture of his life, which was horrible, and of his own soul, hideous in its ugliness. Yet a new day had now dawned for that life and soul; and he seemed to see Satan bathed in the light of Paradise.

How long did he stay weeping? What did he then do and where did he go? We do not know. But it is said that on that same night the stage-driver from Grenoble, passing through the cathedral square in Digne at three in the morning, saw in the shadows the figure of a man kneeling in an attitude of prayer outside the door of Monsieur Bienvenu. (pp. 117-118)

At the end of Part One, Book Two, Valjean is reborn. While maintaining the physical attributes of the former convict, he takes a new identity, a new personality, a new sensitivity to God and to his soul's journey.

Once such moments have occurred, inaction no longer becomes an appropriate choice; it is impossible to choose not to choose.

> ...there could be no middle way for him, that he must become either the best of men or the worst, rise even higher than the bishop himself or sink lower than the felon, reach supreme heights of goodness or become a monster of depravity. (p. 116)

Once he accepts the bishop's offer of love, the hatred which has dominated his psyche for nineteen years begins to melt and slowly becomes impossible. Yes, maintain Hugo and the composers, "such things," such transformations can be because "those moments of blinding and yet frighteningly calm insight" do occur "when the thought goes so deep that it passes beyond reality" (p. 117). Again with Allchin:

> There are so many ways in which God comes to meet us and so many ways in which we may meet him in response. In all the mysteries of love, in all that reveals him to us, we can find the sweetness of his presence. And in all our acts of faith and obedience there is a similar possibility for us to receive him. God draws us to himself....We can, in a measure, draw him to ourselves, by prayer and repentance, by faith and obedience. (*Living Presence of the Past*, p. 68)

For Jean Valjean, the magnitude lies in the discovery of his growing awareness that his own strength is not sufficient, that only God, as first mediated to him by the bishop, is sufficient to help.

In the musical, the Prologue concludes with a moment of transformation and corresponds to the internal events of the long passage cited earlier. The enormous mental agony of Jean Valjean is given concrete substance as "another story must begin." The presence of the bishop becomes not a past event but a present reality which is so explosive that the change it compels both inspires and threatens. It inspires because Valjean feels deeply the power of forgiveness and the promise of reconciliation as the bishop "[touches his] soul and [teaches] him love." Note what Karl Barth has to say about this for all who risk these twin acts.

> Reconciliation is the restitution, the resumption of a fellowship which once existed but was then threatened by dissolution. It is the maintaining, restoring, and upholding of that fellowship in face of an element which disturbs and disrupts and breaks it.

Performing the reconciling work of God, the bishop directs Jean Valjean to begin a journey at the end of which he will discover perfect fellowship with God as he sings "forgive me all my trespasses and take me to your glory." Transformed initially by the bishop, Valjean's focus on God will transform him into the likeness of Christ and to be so transformed is to enter into eternal life.

Yet the presence of the bishop also threatens because it involves for Jean Valjean the need to die to self or, as Saint Paul puts it, "it is no longer I who live but Christ who lives in me." This is what one is called to when one embraces love. The system may threaten to imprison, to reduce one to a number, to place men such as Valjean "upon the rack," "beneath the lash," but the threat must be faced as one becomes more and more his real self even though men like Valjean must be hidden for a while behind aliases like Monsieur le Maire. To paraphrase Cardinal Newman, Valjean's journey will not allow security by a hearth but will plunge him into the world where he will continue to discover what he must seek and where he must "hear the world's witness of it." Remembering Lewis' Orual who must die before she dies and Saint Paul who dies to self in order to live, Hugo uses Valjean to illustrate anew that the whole life has as one of its conditions a death of the self.

Peter Stanhope, a poet and one of the central characters in Charles Williams's *Descent Into Hell*, responds to the tempting offer of Lily Sammile, "but I don't see why you don't enjoy yourselves," with the spiritually powerful insight that "sooner or later, there isn't anything to enjoy in oneself." It is as if Hugo anticipated such an expression as Valjean begins now to reject the love of self which is sinful because it proclaims a center whose end is the soul's death. To refuse the self in such a way is to refuse to descend into hell, to say No to the subtle offer to prefer and enjoy the self, and instead to regain a clear vision of God and the reality of what relationship with him implies. It is to choose to be an integral part in the one story that really matters, to play one's role in the drama as best as one can. Thus when Jean Valjean kneels weeping before the door of the bishop, when he sings "I'll escape now from the world, from the world of Jean Valjean. Jean Valjean is nothing now. Another story must begin" at the end of the Prologue, he chooses to live out the story which the bishop has begun for him, a story which will be an exercise in faith.

The subsequent acts in Valjean's life demonstrate the theological truth that faith is an act of trust, that it gives to us a joy that arises solely from the knowledge that "in God we live and move and have our being." The story that now begins for Jean Valjean will have the opportunity to expand to its true dimension and as others participate in that story we become aware that the disparate elements of human history can be evident in a single life, that the seemingly small room of Valjean's soul can embrace the entire universe by virtue of his decision to love.

Temple remarks that the "Lord calls us to absolute perfection; but he points us here and now to what is for each one the next step...on the way to it" (*Readings in John's Gospel*, p. 227). Valjean has heard the call and now begins to discover that such things as trust, as being called "brother," and as being "claimed for God above" can indeed be. He will hear the words of the bishop over and over and their sound will play upon his being and dominate his mind because the power and love in the words are sufficient to move his will as he feels his shame, discovers his soul, and permits God to move his life in another direction.

As opposed to the arena of pain which he endured as part of the chain gang, Valjean has first discovered through the bishop a widening sphere or arena of love because the spirit of God manifests itself in the world. The world that always hated him, the world that has left him with nothing "but the cry of [his] hate, the cries in the dark that nobody hears," the world that has given him a number and "left [him] for dead just for stealing a mouthful of bread" now can begin to be perceived as God's world, grace and nature somehow, miraculously, intersecting and interpenetrating at every moment. This is an integral part of the new story that "must begin," one which demands a journey to Calvary, a recognition that if there is no cross there is no crown, if the pilgrim is to be able to return home.

At the end of Part One Book Two in the novel and the Prologue in the musical, Valjean's Yes to the bishop and to God has blinded and dazed him and set him out to start all over again. He has surrendered to love and now his journey will embrace the bishop's hope for him as paradoxically he forgets and embraces simultaneously who he was and gets on with the process of becoming who he is. In his commitments to Fantine and Cosette and the poor, he will begin to develop the necessary spiritual equipment so that ultimately he will discover the joy that is offered and accessible to him. The journey to discovery and to his true home will expose him to unimagined ordeals and temptations. As Unamuno writes,

> Those who believe they believe in God, but without passion
> in the heart, without anguish of mind, without uncertainty,
> without doubt and even at times without despair, believe
> only in the idea of God, not in God himself.

Because Valjean believes in God himself, because he is willing to risk an ever-deepening love, because he is willing to engage in spiritual struggle and participate in the Passion of Christ, and because he will venture in faith as he begins his new story, God will continue to call to Valjean through Fantine, Fauchelevant, Cosette, Marius, and even Javert so that he will rise out of his nothingness and accept God's invitation to be someone. The hunger for reality which begins during the course of his encounter with the bishop and ends with his weeping before the bishop's door has taken hold of him and now the new story begins, the one which will complete the restoration of the divine image in Jean Valjean and which will shatter every impulse to anger, hatred, and vengeance.

Chapter 3

The Dream Shattered (Apparently): the Poor, Fantine, and the Abyss

At the end of "The Prologue," Jean Valjean's life is tempestuous, a swirling eddy of emotions signaled by the intensity of the music and the act of shredding his yellow ticket of leave. The music which follows shifts abruptly, the play proper begins, and the poor advance toward the audience, bearing down on it like a tidal wave pronouncing judgment. "Wake up" the music seems to shout and we are asked to be alert to a range of experience from which we might easily have isolated ourselves.

The rhythmic repetition of the first line, "at the end of the day," throughout the number leads to a series of excruciating conclusions: age is a weariness which advances all too quickly; life excludes and chills rather than embraces and warms; such wretchedness is "one day less to be living" and "one day nearer to dying." The cadence imposes on the audience a sensitivity, says to one that closed eyes must be opened, that blinders must be removed, and that being human means to be preparedly alive to the existence of others, especially the wretched of the earth.

The movement of the destitute on the stage is such that they threaten to become one with the audience. Two steps forward, a step in retreat, two more steps, another retreat, until one cannot help but be directed toward Hugo's belief that the wretched of the earth are not relegated to a dim past in a distant country but remain an integral part of our present condition. The "hunger in the land" is not endemic but epidemic, symbolic of a wider hunger which can be quenched now only by those like Valjean who immerse themselves in the poor's plight, and quenched ultimately only by the "bread" and "wine" about which the bishop speaks. For the poor, the outcast, the wretched, death is always proximate because the "righteous hurry past" and are deaf to the "little ones crying."

We wonder today, perhaps at any moment in history, what claim the poor have on us and Hugo provides an answer: perhaps none, other than their poverty, other than the imminence of death, other than the horrible and terrifying fact that they are with us always and somehow, in their presence, measure us in terms of what and how we give. Jean Valjean serves as an archetype of converted love and generosity as he immerses himself in their lives and refuses to keep himself safe at a distance. He gives freely because he has received so from the bishop; he provides work in a factory which is a model for its time. Yet one chooses frequently to ignore Hugo's argument that the voice of the poor must be heard and never cease to be heard. To stop up our ears is to ignore our complicity in rendering such individuals less than human, worthless creatures whose ill fortune is to be caught in "a struggle," in "a war."

The poor sing to those who read the novel, who sit in the orchestra or in the mezzanine at the theater, or who relax in comfort, feet extended toward the fire, drink in hand, senses directed toward tapes and compact discs. We are the "righteous [who] hurry past" and neglect to "hear the little ones crying" as the "winter [comes] on fast ready to kill." The song emits an odor. A graduate student of mine compared it to the smell of the E train in the New York City subway system at three o'clock in the morning, the train ridden by the city's homeless, ragged and filthy. Such poverty imposes itself on one's body as the poor are shrouded in rags, on one's mind as each day draws the poor closer to death, and on one's moral principles as the tenets which ought to govern existence disintegrate so that graft and prostitution become necessary.

For Hugo certainly and perhaps for those involved in the musical, engagement with the poor is first hand, an intimate encounter and such a meeting has the power to set in motion their imaginations and our imaginative responses so that life comes to consciousness within reader and audience. The poor, individually and collectively, move toward the apron of the stage and depict with horror the brutalities with which they must live. The effect is cumulative, a kind of continuous descent into the hell of destitution. As we look at the poor, we see wraiths, a conglomerate of shrunken humanity, who threaten to wither and die and then vanish so that at the end of the evening we have forgotten them. We, who need to engage them, back away and see story rather than reality and thus the too costly price exacted by possible involvement is not considered.

A new cliche has arisen in the last decade of the twentieth century, "been there; done that," which threatens to relegate the past to the past, to immerse in the subconscious of the individual (or deaden altogether) any engagement with what has been or is now an insult to prosperity or propriety. However, Jean Valjean is Hugo's alternative to such a perspective. As a consequence of his about face, for which the bishop acts as the catalyst, and his invention of a new and cheaper clasp for paste jewelry, a bit of hope is able to radiate from even the abyss of gloom and despair until even that ray is shattered by gossip and mistrust. As factory head and subsequently mayor of Montreuil-sur-mer, Valjean becomes Hugo's symbol for those who refuse steadfastly to disengage themselves from the wretched, to be detached from a world of which they are always a part. Thrust forward on his journey by the present fact of the Bishop of Digne, Valjean continues to re-define himself by virtue of how he acts in "this new world" he has chosen to enter.

Though Valjean's prosperity is not accounted for in the musical, it is presented as a given. In the novel, Hugo tells us that Jean Valjean arrived in Montreuil-sur-mer with very little money and an idea for a "simpler and less expensive form of clasp for such things as bracelets" (p. 155) which he put into practice with the happy result that he "had grown rich, which is good, and spread prosperity around him, which is better" (p. 155). Called into a new order by the bishop who has bought his soul and given it to God, Valjean responds in such a way that one perceives his acts, though done at a particular moment in history, as acts into which the eternal enters as well as acts which are gathered up into eternity.

The grace of God meets the transformed desires and work of Valjean so that one begins to comprehend the way in which the past can be changed by the present (*The Living Presence of the Past*, pp. 43-44). Valjean had become Le pere Madeleine, who "had become Monsieur Madeleine, and Monsieur Madeleine had become Monsieur le Maire" (p. 159). Trusted and respected, he functions as a kind of Old Testament judge, raised up by the people and elevated in their midst.

> People came from twenty miles around to consult Monsieur Madeleine. He resolved disputes, prevented law-suits, reconciled enemies. Every man trusted him to judge fairly, as though his guiding spirit were a book of natural law. It was like an epic of veneration spreading, in a matter of six or seven years, throughout the province. (p. 163)

A society in a small town dominated by rot and spiritual death is re-born because of Valjean's redemptive and creative power manifested in his acts as factory owner and mayor.

Hugo smells death in the cities and towns of France because he is alive to it and to what happens in them. Yet he is also awake simultaneously to the reality that a man who is penitent will bring to the life of the poor a sense of engagement which affirms the personal involvement of the individual. The factory might easily be a vehicle for mere accumulation of wealth and the production of more profit and power for the already rich. However, Valjean rejects such a vision because he has begun to see the world sacramentally and has refused to contribute to its pollution. For the poor to live in a world of waste must be repudiated. To participate in such degradation is to disfigure and mar the order of creation. Thus Valjean embraces the needs of the hungry and refuses to treat them as playthings of passion, as automatons to be used merely to satisfy the appetites of the rich on demand.

Valjean looks after the poor, but the poor are so immersed in their own hell that they look out only for themselves: "And there's trouble for all/When there's trouble for one." Hence the treatment of Fantine, whose life has been reduced to less than mediocrity. By "the end of the day," the wretched have been reduced to the condition of prisoners awaiting execution and we discover in them the gradual draining away of life, but Fantine's plight is even worse.

Thenardier has raised the price of caring for Cosette and Fantine has been plunged into despair. The daily routine has reduced her to this—an absence of spirit punctuated by ennui. Fantine is thrust into the metaphorical depths of hell, measured by the self-righteousness of the gossip, Madame Victurnien, for whom life and meaning are absent.

> There are persons whose malice is prompted by the sheer need to gossip. Their conversation—drawing-room chatter, antechamber asides—resembles a wide hearth of the kind that rapidly burns up logs. They need plenty of fuel and their fuel is their neighbor. (p. 172)

Fantine is dismissed – "Right, my girl. On your way." For Madame Victurnien, life is nothing more than a shrewish outburst because her lack of charity and compassion pales beside Fantine's essential goodness and innocence. Hugo accentuates this.

> Madame Victurnien, seeing her pass beneath her window and noting the wretched condition of the 'creature' who thanks to her public spirit had been 'put in her place,' was highly gratified. The cruel of heart have their own black happiness. (p. 175)

Those who are complicit in Fantine's dismissal consider themselves moral and pious, but they lack any understanding of the true implications of such principles; they murder the dream to which one dares to cling.

Though Part I of *Les Miserables* is titled "Fantine," she does not make her initial appearance until Book Three, at which point she begins to function more as a powerful and sympathetic symbol than as a fully realized character. A few pages into the chapter which introduces her, Hugo prepares the reader for the way in which the self-indulgent sexual appetite will consume first and then murder the dream which innocence and beauty dares to envision, and willfully relegate such a victim to the ash heaps of society, discarded as a piece of garbage, and abandoned to a life of degradation and humiliation.

Beautiful and pure, endowed with a dowry of golden hair and teeth of pearl, Fantine had gone to Paris "to seek her fortune" (p. 125) and had become one of a group of four young women. The three older ones were "more experienced, more heedless, and more versed in the ways of the world than Fantine la Blonde, who was encountering her first illusion" (p. 123). The word "illusion" is echoed by Hugo several pages later: "Take heed of what I say, Fantine—I, Tholomyes, am an illusion....But she is not even listening, lost in her golden-head dreams" (p. 137), dreams hatched in Fantine's immersion in the Latin quarter, "swarming with students and grisettes, [which sees] the beginning of the dream" (p. 125).

Such a hope is grounded in innocence and beauty. Having "sprung from the nethermost depths of society" (p. 125), Fantine is without family and identified only by her name, one "bestowed on her by some passer-by who had seen her running barefoot in the streets" (p. 125). She is a melody, a tune looking for accompaniment, and so she falls in love with Felix Tholomyes: "For him it was a passing affair, for her the love of her life" (p. 125). The mere phrase "passing affair" defines accurately the nature of any relationship in which one person treats another as an object. All Tholomyes desires is the pleasure which Fantine can provide and though he amuses himself with her for a short time, he illustrates precisely what C. S. Lewis defines in *The Four Loves* as sexual desire without Eros. Tholomyes wants merely the thing in itself, the sensory pleasure, without Fantine. He wants "a pleasure for which a woman happens to be the necessary piece of apparatus. How much [Tholomyes] cares about [Fantine] as such may be gauged by his attitude to her five minutes after fruition [one does not keep the carton after one has smoked the cigarettes]" (*The Four Loves*, p. 135).

Tholomyes, completely unlike Marius whose love for Cosette will be defined by purity of devotion, "[robs] the melody from [Fantine's] heart" (p. 845) and thus what remains is a shell, a shadow, an emptiness of despair. Alan Ecclestone captures the nature of Fantine's poverty, imposed carelessly by Tholomyes, when he writes in *Yes to God* that "passion without engagement [runs] recklessly to waste, but passion engaged with fantasy such as has inspired the generation of 'Playboy' could have no consequence but the desolation of spirit and a widening of the estrangement between men and women" (*Yes to God*, p. 95). Such use, even abuse, yields waste and Fantine, overwhelmed by the gallant Tholomyes, has a child, weeps bitterly when abandoned, goes to work in Jean Valjean's factory, and is unfairly dismissed. In the musical, the sequence of events prompts the depressingly haunting "I Dreamed a Dream."

Fantine, reduced to an object without a real identity, is captured in her despair by Herbert Kretzmer who uses the past tense throughout the song to accentuate what has happened to Fantine: life has the power to murder or shatter the dream, especially when the dream is anchored in something false, no matter how pure or innocent the attachment may be.

> Although, alas, she would have refused Tholomyes nothing, her expression in repose was above all virginal....Love, let us agree, may be a fault. Fantine's was the innocence that rides above it. (p. 129)

The explosion of Fantine's dream is conveyed in the lyrics through the repetition of "was." A time must have existed when the dream could have issued in hope fulfilled, but when Fantine sings she musters all that she can of herself, to be truly herself, to express the agony which lies within.

The agony has caused her to fall out with the spiritual world. She acts and sings as if the world which has shattered her dream is a world from which God has chosen either to absent himself or to hold himself aloof from entering into the misfortunes of his creatures. The God who enters creation in the person of Christ is perceived by Fantine to withhold forgiveness and when such a perception exists, no matter how inaccurate, then the result is to live in hell.

"I Dreamed a Dream" becomes a desperate song which acts as a soliloquy and shares with the audience the occasions of hope for joy and the resultant sorrow, perplexity, and fear, that have entered Fantine's life. The song notices and interprets whatever she, in her despair, has come to know of hope and faith and pity and love. The longings and desires she has had—the kindness of men, the innocence and purity of love, the harmony of the world's tune—have been thwarted by that universe which appears hostile yet which bears witness to the presence of God in the midst of even the most severe agonies, though she does not yet recognize this presence.

The estranged and alienated Fantine tries desperately to articulate her predicament. The oxymoron "soft as thunder" accentuates the metaphorical "tigers" who shred dreams and lead one to "shame." Indeed, Schoenberg and Boublil compose in such a way that "shame" is extended, rising in the register so that the despair is felt deeply within. One senses the depth of Fantine's vulnerability and the sympathetic symbolic figure of the novel is raised out of the symbolic mode and made entirely human. She bears witness to the reality of life's brutality and danger, its ability to pierce our dreams and personal defenses.

Employed and then fired, Fantine sings of the remnant of the dream, but a subtle irony exists within the words. The "he" of whom she dreams turns out not to be Tholomyes but Christ, or Christ in the form of Jean Valjean. It is he who will snatch her out of the jaws of the tiger of despair and empower her to face what lies ahead. Frozen spiritually and seemingly bankrupt morally, hell appears to be all that life offers Fantine. The dream appears to be shattered, but that will not be the case.

The dismissal of Fantine is, unfortunately, not the end of her story. Her dream destroyed, her hopes quite undone, Fantine has begun her descent into the abyss. First a pauper, she sells her hair and her teeth, a degradation that makes her nearly unrecognizable, an act in order to save her sick child, an act at the mercy of the predatory Thenardiers.

> Fantine turned her cropped head and it seemed that she had aged ten years overnight…the candle lighted her face. It was a bloodstained smile. There were flecks of blood at the corners of her mouth and a wide gap between her upper lip (p. 178).

The destitute are no longer as far away as they seemed when she was with Tholomyes and certainly no longer on the fringe as when she worked at the factory; she is now one with them and in that abyss of destitution she is left with only a single alternative if Cosette is to survive: "She became a prostitute" (p. 179).

For Hugo, slavery, thought to have been erased from European civilization, still exists in the form of prostitution and afflicts women where it "preys on grace, frailty, beauty, motherhood" (p. 180). He images prostitution as a kind of disintegration, a rotting away at the core of what marks a woman as human. The prostitute is no longer able to see and to touch things in such a way that would permit her to keep pace with the deepest needs of her life.

In the musical, the grotesque nature of prostitution is somewhat camouflaged by the oxymoronic "lovely ladies" of the red light district. For these women who have become dirt, their currency is their bodies, their exchange rate is set by the pimp, and the traffic is merely the commodity of sex, what Grossman calls "the promiscuous intermingling of bodies without names" (p. 64). Prostitute and customer are dehumanized; she exists as nothing more than the necessary piece of apparatus for his momentary animal desire. Each has become a mere vehicle for excess and release.

The flurry of activity on the stage, the lively staccato of the music, and the costuming, make-up, and dramatic sexual thrusts as the sailors' "anchor[s]" are deposited in the "whores' harbor[s]" can mask an essential hunger and, if one is not careful, does not heed the signals, the response elicited may very well be more that of humor than of revulsion. But no doubt exists as to what Hugo intended and what applies to Fantine applies to the prostitute in general, no matter how she is disguised or made to feel respectable. No matter what the circumstances, she is the "unmoving countenance of the dishonored" (p. 182).

The dominant imagery in the novel and the musical is that of violence because that is what prostitution is: an act of violence, of abuse to the body, mind, and soul. On the stage, the "lovely ladies" cannot conceal their vitiated state as they "[wait] for a bite" from their evening customers who will enjoy their traffic at "bargain prices" with "extra" added if the act takes too long. And the whores have no difficulty defining their customers; they make no attempt to sanitize the essence of those whom they engage: "harbor rats and alley cats and every kind of scum."

Such an existence grows increasingly more blind and more insensitive to the world in which it lives. It become callous and lost, "resigned with the resignation that resembles indifference as death resembles sleep" (p. 182). It reduces Fantine to a mere shadow of what she was, someone who no longer "seeks to escape from anything" (p. 182), someone who, in the musical, picks up the strains of "I Dreamed a Dream" and sings plaintively and then shrilly "Easy money/Lying on a bed/Just as well they never see the hate/That's in your head!/Don't they know/They're making love to one already dead?" In short, prostitution renders the one who provides the service a corpse and the one who makes use of it a necrophiliac, at least metaphorically.

However, while Fantine's need to turn to prostitution disfigures her and causes her to become a symbol of the misery which engulfs such individuals, it also provides the means for her redemption. Life has indeed "dropped [Fantine] at the bottom of the heap," such is the position assigned the whore, but, like Dostoyevsky's Sonia in *Crime and Punishment* and William Kennedy's Helen Archer in *Ironweed*, she never attempts to delude herself about her repulsive existence and thus her encounter with Bamatabois allows her to retain the smallest thread of dignity and pride.

Based on a true incident witnessed by Hugo, Fantine's encounter with the supposed gentleman, Bamatabois, particularizes what has been merely general. It is a meeting with a monster, a hideous creature who torments Fantine "with a fresh sally reflecting on her looks, her attire, and anything else that occurred to him" (p. 182), an ogre who sees his prey as a thing which he will sample because the customer is entitled to see "what he gets in advance." No matter what the era, no matter how the customer attempts to disguise himself in some sort of cloak of respectability, and no matter whether the culture or the government condones the activity of "[gentlemen] of orthodox opinions" who are "elegant idlers" (p. 182), they remain monsters, "bastards," "rats." Similarly, no matter whether the woman is a well-dressed member of a high society escort service or someone who is shriveled and worn by life on the street, Hugo argues that she (Fantine in particular, the prostitute in general) remains a "sad and garish ghost" (p. 182), a mere shell of what she was intended to be.

Hugo's observations on prostitution are as relevant now as at any moment in history. They reflect what Allchin calls the "powerful sense of disintegration which afflicts our society." These women have forgotten how to see and touch things in a manner which would permit them to actualize what is most needed in their lives. However, for Fantine, all is not lost because the riddle of her shredded destiny is solved by Jean Valjean as he procures her freedom over and against the protest of Javert.

For Hugo in *Les Miserables*, God is the only one who knows the answer to all things and God, mediated through the re-born Valjean, becomes a present reality in the seemingly helpless plight of Fantine. As C. S. Lewis points out in *The Problem of Pain*, the prostitute is in no danger of finding her life so palatable that she will be unable to turn to God or recognize him when He comes (p. 87). The man whom she had once venerated and who then had become inadvertently responsible for her shattered existence now re-appears as her savior, the man who comes "from God in heaven," and she is ready to embrace him. Unlike the proud, arrogant, and self-righteous Bamatabois or the avaricious Thenardiers to whom she has entrusted Cosette, her soul is not in the danger which one might imagine.

One will recall Valjean's transformation discussed earlier. His subsequent acts as mayor are a consequence of the active presence of God's love in his heart. Whatever and whenever he gives to the poor, he remembers what he was and what the bishop did for him. In a sense, his life becomes his prayer and as a consequence he is able to bear Fantine's initial hatred of him.

Indeed, he is able to absorb it because identification with the despised is recognized and acknowledged. The man whom Fantine first believes to be mocking her becomes angelic, speaking in the tones of an angel in opposition to the voice of a demon which emanates from Javert. To her hopeless plea, "if there's a God above," Valjean supplies the answer: yes, and in the midst of horror and brutality He does not absent himself from his creation. In the abyss, Fantine discovers a beam of hope and thus begins her journey toward salvation.

Valjean says to her "you have suffered very greatly, my poor child, but you must not complain for now you have your recompense. This is how men create saints, and it is useless to blame them because they cannot do otherwise. The hell you have endured is the doorway to Heaven, through which you had to pass" (p. 191). Sunk into prostitution solely for the sake of her child and rescued by one who has had his soul saved from black thoughts and given to God, the engagement between prostitute and former convict opens them to a future in which light will cleave darkness, good will triumph over evil, and the power of God will continue to redeem the most wretched the earth has to offer.

Chapter 4

Jean Valjean's Soliloquy:
The Tempestuous Price of Self-Discovery

One of the longest and most pivotal Books in *Les Miserables* is "The Champmathieu Affair" (Part I, Book Seven). At this point in the narrative, his true identity masked, Jean Valjean appears to be safely and respectably ensconced as the mayor of Montreuil-sur-mer, admired by all, his past neatly buried. Yet it is now that his security is threatened suddenly as Javert reveals to him that the convict Jean Valjean has been arrested and is due to come before the court. What follows this announcement is a psychological struggle which is as intense as one can find in literature, a conflict so protracted and theologically subtle, so exclusively mental, that one sees and feels the destiny of Valjean's soul hanging in the balance. The battle is dramatized in the novel through the metaphor of a tempest and in the musical through a question which, when answered, can lead only to condemnation or damnation. What transpires ultimately will confirm and validate Valjean's decision to reject the secure and comfortable surroundings of his new life as mayor in order to save not only his soul but also his life.

In Chapter III of Book Seven, "A tempest in a human skull," Valjean's memory is kindled and he recollects his past slowly and painfully not yet knowing that such an act will place him ultimately under the saving embrace of God.. Hugo expresses imaginatively the storm within thus:

To make a poem of the human conscience, even in terms of a single man and the least of men, would be to merge all epics in a single epic transcending all. Conscience is the labyrinth of illusion, desire, and pursuit, the furnace of dreams, the repository of thoughts of which we are ashamed; it is the pandemonium of sophistry, the battlefield of passions. To peer at certain moments into the withdrawn face of a human being in the act of reflection, to see something of what lies beyond their outward silence, is to discern struggle on a Homeric scale, conflicts of dragons and hydras, aerial hosts as in Milton, towering vistas as in Dante. The infinite space that each man carries within himself, wherein despairingly he contrasts the movements of his spirit with the acts of his life, is an overpowering thing. (p. 208)

To claim that a struggle such as Jean Valjean's exists on "a Homeric scale" may appear hyperbolic except when one realizes that the stakes are one's soul. As he wrestles with those false perceptions of reality and illusion which compete with truth, Valjean shares a hard fellowship with other literary figures like Dostoyevsky's Raskolnikov, Conrad's Jim and Nostromo, C. S. Lewis' Ransom, Charles Williams's Wentworth, and Shakespeare's tragic heroes as he discovers that the imagination has the dual capacity not only to enlighten but also to deceive. For Jean Valjean, the end result is that as a man in the process of conversion he wills to risk the struggle in the heart of the tempest because his deepest desire is to be whole and thus he becomes "a changed man, enacting in his life what the bishop had sought to make of him. It was more than a transformation; it was a transfiguration" (p. 208).

Because the change was a "transfiguration," because any such change deemed thus shares in the transfiguration of Christ, the consequence is that Valjean gains his freedom, that he is able to discern who he truly is because he is willing to risk the encounter with God. He chooses to embrace a perception of reality which exists, in Eliot's language, at the intersection of time and the timeless, at the still point of the turning world, at the intersection of sinner and saint, and what emerges is a man whose life flows from the "appropriation of his identity in relation to God."

Similarly, in the musical, "Who Am I?" functions as a means to an end, a means of confronting and dealing with the things life brings and of making some sense of living. In the process, in the novel and in the musical, Valjean is alone with God and in his terrible solitude he chooses to go down into the depths of his being, to get in touch with that essential self whose blindness has been healed by the bishop, where he discovers that God cannot be put off with speculation about the dependence of a town and its factory workers. It is here that he commences to grasp what F. D. Maurice meant when he wrote that "'He descended into hell' affirms that there is no corner of God's universe over which his love has not brooded." The merely rational approach would permit him to stand aside, but the imaginative approach compels him to participate. He is able to hold before himself what it means to be lost and forsaken, blind and lame, rich and haughty, proud and strong.

Such a journey toward freedom is never easy; indeed, it is much more often a kind of crucifixion, what Kretzmer identifies as this "never-ending road to Calvary." Hugo expresses the journey in this way.

> Apart from their strict underlying religious intention, his every act until that day had been for the purpose of digging a hole in which his real name might be buried. What he had most feared, in his moments of recollection and his wakeful nights, was to hear that name spoken. He had said to himself that the rebirth of that name would for him mean the end of everything, the destruction of the new life he had built, even—who could tell?—of the new soul he had fashioned. The thought alone, the very possibility, made him shudder. Had anyone told him that the day would come when the name, the hideous words 'Jean Valjean,' would suddenly resound in his ears like a thunderclap, coming like a blaze of light out of darkness to tear aside the mystery in which he had disguised himself; and had they gone on to tell him that this would be no threat unless he chose to make it so, that the light would serve merely to deepen his disguise and that the worthy Monsieur Madeleine, being confronted with the

ghost of Jean Valjean, might emerge from the encounter even more honoured and secure than before—had anyone said this to him he would have stared in amazement, thinking the words insane. Yet this was precisely what had happened, this heaping-up of impossibilities was a fact; God had allowed the fantasy to become a reality. (pp. 211-212)

The tempest within becomes an agonizing process of self-examination and such scrutiny identifies the trouble which lies at the center of Valjean's existence. As Kenneth Leech notes in *True Prayer*, the one who is so inclined dares to strip bare his spirit and tackle falsehood. The entire process "involves wrestling and conflict, not a mechanical formalism" (p. 142). It is a kind of Lenten pilgrimage as one moves from discovery through observation to a point of discovery through participation.

Such wrestling involves the decision to openness, to the rejection of easy justifications for one's possible behavior. After all, Valjean could pretend easily that he "[did] not see [Champmathieu's] agony." What intervenes? What determines the moral decisions that one must make? Often, as with Jean Valjean, the answer lies in a vision, an imaginative yet real and true awareness of a presence, in Valjean's case that of the bishop, "more urgent than in life" (p. 214). Aided by his own integrity and the bishop's presence, Valjean begins to discover that he will be able to pay the terrible price, that he can express with honesty and without fear who he is. He can choose to sing the song, to join in the dance, to "tune the instrument of his heart" and hence discover that the "quality of eternity" is mediated by the willingness to make the wager of faith. Such a decision gives Valjean his nobility because he accepts the consequences for affirming who he really is. Though the passage is lengthy, it is best to let Hugo speak for Valjean at this point.

He pursued his self-questioning, severely demanding what he had meant when he said, "My object is achieved." Certainly his life had a purpose, but was it simply to hide himself, to outwit the police? Had everything he had done been for no better reason than this? Had he not had a greater purpose, the saving not of his life but of his soul, the

resolve to become a good and honourable and upright man
as the bishop required of him—had not that been his true
and deepest intention? Now he talked of closing the door
on the past when, God help him, he would be reopening the
door by committing an infamous act, not merely that of a
thief but of the most odious of thieves. He would be robbing
a man of his life, his peace, his place in the sun, morally
murdering him by condemning him to the living death that
is called a convict prison. But if, on the other hand, he saved
the man by repairing the blunder, by proclaiming himself
Jean Valjean the felon, this would be to achieve his own
true resurrection and firmly close the door on the hell from
which he sought to escape. To return to it in appearance
would be to escape from it in reality. This is what he must
do, and without it he would have accomplished nothing, his
life would be wasted, his repentance meaningless, and there
would be nothing left for him to say except, "Who cares?" He
felt the presence of the bishop, more urgent than in life; he
felt the old priest's eyes upon him and knew that henceforth
Monsieur Madeleine the mayor, with all his virtues, would
seem to be abominable, whereas Jean Valjean the felon would
be admirable and pure. Other men would see the mask, but
the bishop would see the face; others would see the life, but
he would see the soul. So there was nothing for it but to go
to Arras and rescue the false Jean Valjean by proclaiming
the true one. The most heartrending of sacrifices, the most
poignant of victories, the ultimate, irretrievable step—but it
had to be done. It was his most melancholy destiny that he
could achieve sanctity in the eyes of God only by returning
to degradation in the eyes of men. (p. 214)

Here we see that hard work which accompanies the soul's
pilgrimage toward a life that will be holy and a heart that is true to
the vision that has been embraced. Here is a soul which aches to
be filled, to be gathered in and held forever. It is a soul which seeks
desperately to deny that view which becomes pervasive at some
point in any generation: that the self is all that matters and that the
Gospel paradox of losing one's life in order to gain it is an illusion
at best, a delusion at worst. Valjean's decision marks a radical

step in his journey toward resurrection and it is necessitated by a dramatic shift in his perspective, though not so final as it first appears in the passage above.

Important theological truths are at work here, ones which will be tested repeatedly in this affair and beyond. Hugo and Kretzmer grasp that for the pilgrim like Jean Valjean self-knowledge is essential to a response to Christ's invitation to follow him, to take up one's cross and repudiate the justifications offered by the world, and to live completely and with courage. Having decided, having arrived at the awareness that while he does not know what lies ahead but does know *Who*, Valjean perceives "that this was the second turning-point in his spiritual life and in his destiny: the bishop had been the first, and the man Champmathieu marked the second. This was the ultimate crisis, the final trial of his fortitude" (p. 215).

Yet on the heels of affirmation and apparent final solution arrive doubt and multiple possibilities for remaining silent. A kind of voluble alter ego attempts to persuade him to mortgage his soul and freedom in the name of security and safety—Champmathieu is not so important; Valjean is necessary for the people of Montreuil-sur-mer; Fantine will sink into despair. He even considers burning the bishop's candlesticks until a voice rises within him and shatters the carefully manufactured rationalizations of his voluble self. "Take good heed!" says this voice. "The blessings will fall away before they are heard in Heaven, and only the curse will reach God" (p. 220).

In the musical, which captures succinctly the inner agony which torments Valjean, the puzzle is defined by two pairs of questions, each one punctuated by the exclamatory "If I speak I am condemned/If I stay silent I am damned!" As he struggles to identify himself, to answer the tempestuous question "Who am I?" he recognizes the need to accept the wilderness road, to acknowledge the desert inherent in the number 24601. His refusal to hide that identity from himself or others commences another resurrection experience. He grasps the subtle distinction between "condemned" and "damned," between the agony of the present which will end and the torment of an eternity which has no end.

Hugo captures the enormity of the struggle as he links Jean Valjean with Christ.

> Thus he strove in torment as another man had striven eighteen hundred years before him, the mysterious Being in whom were embodied all the saintliness and suffering of mankind. He too while the olive-leaves quivered around him, had again and again refused the terrible cup of darkness urged upon him beneath a sky filled with stars. (p. 221)

In his decision to name himself, 24601 becomes secondary, a fact but one which has lost the power to devour the one who admits to this part of his dark past. Such an act derives solely from God who "gave [him] hope when hope was gone [and] gave [him] strength to journey on." What is true now will remain true as he continues his journey. Whatever hell he may descend into in this world will be accompanied by the implicit recognition that Christ has descended before him and that in whatever dangers he faces Christ will be there to raise him up. In his own way, he might very well utter some form of this Celtic prayer.

> In the storms of life,
> In the sinking of the disciple,
> In the scorning and rejecting,
> In the betrayals and denials,
> In the hells and crucifixions,
> In the ebbing out of life,
> Christ beneath me.
> And I know that You are the Risen Lord of Life.
> (*Border Lands*, p. 103)

Valjean's desire that he not be tested is perfectly legitimate, but in the test he discovers that God meets him in the horrors rather than enabling him to escape them. The implication is clear: the more one grasps the truth of Augustine's principle that the heart will find no rest until it rests in God the more readily one will decide to affirm God and, as a consequence, to engage life with honor and integrity. In the process, the individual discovers the nature of genuine goodness. It is not that the storms and struggles will be avoided or escaped—more may arise than before—or that one will never have the sense that he is perishing, but that in the midst of the tempest will arise the certainty that God loves and cares. This discovery will delineate ultimately the steps Valjean will take in his journey toward salvation—his generosity toward the poor, his belief in Fantine, his rescue of Marius and surrender of Cosette, his forgiveness of Javert—and it will be accompanied by an ever-deepening sense that in "this frail craft that we call life [God] is present" and that "He does not want us to be overcome" (*Border Lands*, p. 164).

"A tempest in a human skull" and "Who Am I?" are a journey into the heart of the mystery of salvation, into the magnitude and glory of God's love as evident on the Cross. In some way, each defines what Valjean has now managed to make of existence, a decision which determines how Valjean is to proceed, and each serves as a catalyst for all subsequent liberating acts. In the struggle Hugo creates for Valjean, the ex-convict illustrates a point made by Alan Ecclestone: as "we strive to know ourselves, we are seeking to know not a speck of dust nor the species man but the Word that was spoken and took our flesh, the Yes that permitted us to be" (*Yes to God*, p. 120).

When Valjean sings "My soul belongs to God, I know/I made that bargain long ago," a bargain he didn't recall having made at the time, but one by which he has tried to abide, he accepts that grace offered by God freely, a gift which transcends spiritual fuel, which becomes what H. A. Williams defines in *True Wilderness* as "the creative quality of life itself—all the things we do, all the things that happen to us...all the splendors and the miseries, all the pleasure and the pain" (p. 55). To believe that one's soul belongs to God is to be awakened to Christ, to his light and love, to his life and purpose. It is to know that one's eyes have been opened to God's presence, one's heart to God's indwelling, one's mind to God's abiding, and one's will to God's guiding (*Border Lands*, p. 16). In another sense, it is what C. S. Lewis identifies as a "real giving up of the self," of throwing "it away blindly so to speak" because Valjean will receive in return a real new self.

The movement here is toward freedom through an act of courage, through the decision to refuse to deny and instead say yes to the suffering and agony which may be part of any existence. To choose the apparent freedom implied in silence is only to remain in chains. For the man who recognizes that his soul belongs to God, the soul becomes equipped for those acts which are agonizing and which have devastating consequences in the present but lead to salvation ultimately. Even in apparent lostness such choice liberates and thus one can bear the condemnation of the moment when one is able to grasp the alternative implications of eternity and what is suggested by the possibility of damnation.

The bishop has enabled Jean Valjean to hear his own name and all that name conveys, and in the midst of his explosive pain he acknowledges that name. Thus he is set free and his journey toward Arras gives him an increased sense of who he truly is. His self-scrutiny, his engagement with multiple voices and conflicting choices, leads to self-knowledge and such awareness, always in the process of being deepened, eventually leads to repentance – "forgive me all my trespasses and take me to your glory" – because we can be penitent only for that which we know and affirm.

As the scene shifts on the stage, the tempest within is actualized before the court in the painful outburst "I'm Jean Valjean!" Dramatically, Valjean rips open the coat and shirt worn by Monsieur Madeleine, the mayor of Montreuil-sur-mer, and unmasks his real identity in a burst of energy: Jean Valjean – 24601. He owns his history and, as Allchin remarks, in such an act one's personal identity not only survives but begins to grow and it is this that allows Valjean to "face the future with hope and a sense of purpose" (*The Living Presence of the Past*, p. 25).

As Valjean declares himself before the Assizes, the reader and theatergoer discover a man in the process of continuing transformation, a man who has dug deep into the recesses of his own heart and peeled away all the casuistry that appeals to a denial of the self, who has begun to see more and more clearly. Hugo and Kretzmer define for us the individual who refuses steadfastly to try to manipulate God's will so that it coincides with his own. What he chooses instead is an act of magnanimity, of greatness of soul, as he surrenders his will to God in a plea that God work in him and through him to accomplish whatever God's purpose is. It is as if God answers his prayer and awakens him to God's light and love, God's life and purpose, and then opens his eyes, his heart, his mind, and his will to God's presence, indwelling, abiding, and guiding (*Border Lands*, p. 16). The consequence, as with anyone who decides to surrender his will to God's will, is finally to desire God's will rather than his own. Finally, in the storm, the individual will place his hand in God's and will be able to pray with Jesus in Gethsemane: "Not my will but thine."

In this crucial chapter in the novel, which functions as an extended interior soliloquy, and in the dramatic stage performance, we discover a man who defines what it cost to choose God as a companion on the journey. He is now able to pray, perhaps something like this.

> Christ, come enter through the door of the past;
> into the remembered and the forgotten,
> into the joys and sorrows,
> into the recording room of memories,
> into the secret room of sin,
> into the hidden room of shame,
> into the mourning room of sorrow,
> into the bright room of love,
> into the joyful room of achievement.
> Come Christ, enter
> into the fiber of [my] being,
> into the conscious and subconscious,
> into the roots of personality.
> Cleanse me from my secret faults and renew a
> right spirit within me. (*Border Lands*, p. 101)

In the decision, God refuses to leave him desolate (as Christ has promised) and the disciple moves toward Calvary and what lies beyond. Light is embraced; he who is the Light of the world is affirmed. Hence, others can be raised to that Light because one man demonstrates that it is possible to renounce what is safe and death-dealing and attest instead that one can live redemptively in the midst of conflict, struggle, and doubt no matter how terrified.

As Valjean stands before the court and announces his decision, we discover the inherent strength which lies in moral rectitude.

> "You who are here present, you find me deserving of pity, do you not? For myself, when I consider what I came so near to doing, I think I am to be envied. But still I wish that none of this had happened." (p. 258)

To have desired God in the midst of confusion and perplexity, to grope in the shadows and darkness, these are signs of what Leech sees as living prayer in a man on the road to redemption (*True Prayer*, p. 68). Having wrestled and prayed, it is no longer a question of escape, only of triumph over those elements which tempt the soul and would lead it to damnation. Such an act is an initial step on the road to clarity of sight and while the world may never understand what has been done, while it may grudge one such new birth and substantial resurrection, while, remaining on the outside, it will be tormented by the inner peace of one who has chosen God and it will be infuriated by his joy, it is crucial that one live in the present memory of what Christ bore on the Cross and, in Valjean's particular case, what the bishop has done for him. Only then can one "die before he dies" and arrive at a point of self-denial and self-acceptance and begin to see himself as he truly is.

Chapter 5

"Out of the Depths I have Called You": Valjean, Fantine, Javert: the Conflict Engaged

Valjean's efforts toward the release of Fantine and the subsequent resolution of his inner torment in the Champmathieu affair are a consequence of his willingness to engage all facets of existence, of his recognition that special moral categories do not exist for the expedience of a given moment. Good and evil exist and are mutually opposed; absolute moral principles are poured into creation for without them what is evil for one would be permissible for another. The catalyst for this series of decisions—for all of his decisions—is his response to the Bishop of Digne and his discovery that such a response cannot be rounded off neatly. Mediated through the life of another, the call of God necessitates an increasing awareness that an initial response demands more and more. As Dietrich Bonhoeffer noted in *The Cost of Discipleship*, Christ bids one come and die, not come and be safe.

Errors of omission there may be, even errors of understanding, and blind spots will need to be healed so that the journey toward salvation can continue. However, no matter what flaws surface in his character in the course of his pilgrimage, Valjean will refuse to permit any individual to fall away unregarded, to neglect to alleviate need no matter the circumstance. Fantine is provided for in the hospital, Fauchlevant, a bitter rival, is rescued from certain death, and Champmathieu is set free in a "state of total stupefaction, thinking all men mad and understanding nothing of what had transpired" (p. 259). Hugo grasps the essential theological point that the testing of one's life, of the philosophical perspective one has chosen to embrace, will rarely appear on a single battlefront for which one has prepared a defense in advance or confine itself to neatly compartmentalized categories which one has experienced already. It is as if, at times, the onslaught occurs at multiple points simultaneously.

In the midst of their painful pilgrimages toward Calvary, redemption, and salvation, without ever stopping to think of what they do as religious acts, Fantine and Valjean define what is meant by intercession: it means "literally to stand between, to become involved in the conflict" (*True Prayer*, p. 25). In another sense, it is to permit glory to break into one's life even though one may not quite be certain of what he has glimpsed. As David Adam points out in *Glimpses of Glory*, all who live upon the earth "are in the heart of God and God is within the heart of every piece of his creation" (p. 3), a truth which Fantine grasps when she sings that Valjean comes from God in heaven. Though Fantine has been humiliated and disfigured by her life as a prostitute, such abject misery arises solely because of her love and concern for Cosette. She is literally "a girl who can't refuse," one who hates what she must do, one whose body is more corpse than living creature, but deep within her she is able to bring to God all that is in her heart—the ache, the pain, the humiliation, the anger, even the little hope that she retains. It is as if she recognizes intuitively that their hearts are one, that she abides in him and He in her.

Similarly, Jean Valjean's theft of the loaf of bread for his sister's starving family, a criminal act driven by desperation and concern for the welfare of others, and later his redemptive works as factory head and mayor illustrate his attempts to cooperate with God in God's work of reconciling a fallen world to himself. In his dangerous journey through the criminal infested mountains, the Bishop of Digne knew the fact of God in his own heart and thus in the heart of anyone he encountered. He recognized this in Jean Valjean as well and Valjean is hence granted a similar vision in all whom he meets. Having become a man whose life is an extended prayer, he is able, even in his fears, to act in the knowledge that even the Thenardiers and Javert are somehow joined in the heart of God. For Valjean, intercession becomes a "method of stopping and getting glimpses of the hidden glory of God" (*Glimpses of Glory*, p. 3).

The extended ministry of reconciliation is an essential part of the process of becoming a new man and it is a process which never ceases. Fear is what demands that Fantine become a prostitute, fear of what will happen to Cosette, but as we see with her and with Valjean fear can never have the same power to direct human conduct and moral choices as does love. We may regard both Fantine and Valjean as powerless, but if we do so we are wrong. We need to be reminded of Charles Williams's dictum that power is not something one has but something one is. Measured by a different standard, by an objective and austere yet gentle love which, when lifted high on a cross draws to it a suffering world, Fantine's love becomes that power which is ultimately not only the means to her own redemption but also to the eventual freedom and joy which is to be Cosette's. Somehow, mystically, even miraculously, all things work together for the glory of God. Similarly, since his love is grounded ultimately in the power of the Cross, Valjean is able to live dynamically and respond as he does because the love of Christ directs him, defines him, even comes to discipline him in every facet of his life because he chooses to follow God in Christ.

When we meet Fantine for the last time in the hospital, this young girl of twenty-five has become no longer the shadow of her former self but its ghost. Hugo writes that "physical deterioration had completed the work of spiritual sickness" (p. 234) and that "disease is a great simulator of age" (p. 234). Her only thread of hope lies in the return of Cosette, but it is a thread which will be cut.

As Fantine nears death, her delirium is imaged perfectly on the bare stage and in the music, which is a reprise of the haunting strains of "I Dreamed a Dream," and captures essentially what transpires in the novel. There she imagines that she can hear

Cosette, even recognize her voice, but it is only another child playing in the yard, someone else's daughter. She lies in bed trembling. Her tormented motherhood wells up inside her and her imagination is unleashed as she engages in an apostrophe with the absent Cosette. All the activities of a child become present to the dying mother who has been denied the joys of mothering: the day of play and games, the tucking into bed when the day is over, the lullaby, the prayers. Now, her arm stretched agonizingly toward her imaginary vision, she sees her daughter coming to her in a series of images which culminate in the desire to protect Cosette from all harm.

> Come to me, Cosette, the night is fading.
> Don't you see the evening star appearing?
> Come to me and rest against my shoulder—
> How fast the minutes fly away and every minute colder.
> Hurry near, another day is dying.
> Don't you hear the winter wind is crying?
> There's a darkness which comes without a warning
> But I will sing you lullabies and wake you in the morning.

As day dies, as darkness invades, Fantine still seeks to protect her child. The "lullabies" she wants desperately to sing function as a kind of compline, as a protective shield which will enfold the child in the hands of God until a new day dawns. Hoping that Monsieur le Maire will bring Cosette to her, she would bind herself and her child to God and him to them in the power of the Trinity. However, such a vision is not to be realized. A chill finally envelops her, the light on the stage fades except for that light which is trained on Fantine, a light which bathes her in the love of God. It is this light which will always cleave the darkness because its origin is not in this world. With the penitent and converted Valjean beside her, Fantine has been able to imagine Cosette in all her glory, to glimpse her as she was intended to be. The vision is that of someone near death, but that cannot rob it of its essential truth because Valjean's love has filled Fantine's emptiness and the void within, the shattered dream and the despair of the prostitute, has been opened to eternity. In the novel, Jean Valjean bends over and speaks to the dead Fantine, and Hugo asks a series of questions: "What did he say to her? What could that man who was condemned say to that woman who was dead? What words did he use? No living person heard them? Did the dead hear them?" (p. 270)

The answers to these questions are given in the novel and in the musical. In the former, Sister Simplice, "the only witness of the scene," described frequently that she "distinctly saw the dawning of a smile on the pallid lips and in the vacant eyes, wide in the astonishment of death" (p.270). In the language of faith and belief, the sister knows from within that the worlds of the living and the dead interpenetrate, that Valjean has access to the newly dead Fantine and she to him.

Meanwhile on stage, Valjean sings to Fantine that Cosette "will live within [his] care," that "[he] will raise her to the light," that he will never desert her. That light, that radiance which has its ground in God, originates for Valjean from the bishop and has become the focus of his existence. The light of God cascades and Valjean's words become not only a promise but a kind of prayer. Music and words combine in such a way that what could be bathetic is not and the final exchange is laden with power. Valjean has been seized by an overwhelming love, one that permits him to assure Fantine that Cosette will live in his protection and that Fantine herself will now be sheltered from the storm. It is a love which arrives in a life-altering whirlwind at Arras and which then manifests itself at the bedside of a dying girl. The "darkness which comes without a warning" now arrives as love and conveys the truth for which Auden longs in these lines from his song about love.

> Just as I'm picking my nose?
> Will it knock at my door in the morning,
> Or tread in the bus on my toes?
> Will it come like a change in the weather?
> Will its greeting be courteous or rough?
> Will it alter my life altogether?

O tell me the truth about love.

For Hugo, the world is a battlefield, not only political but also spiritual, "enemy-occupied territory" as C. S. Lewis wrote, and those who perform on the stage of battle become more and more familiar with the world's darkness: the bishop battled it, ironically, in the prelates of his church, Valjean wars against it as he is first turned away and then hunted, and the poor never lose the sense that it will obliterate any hint or promise of goodness and rescue. Man's supreme need becomes light, the Light of God. Such light can be shed only by those who seek to illuminate what they know to be true: that the love of God cannot be eclipsed. Hence, when Valjean confronts Javert in the hospital and begs for three days to fulfill his pledge to intercede, he recognizes that he is stronger than Javert because there resides within him a power which the inspector cannot comprehend.

For Javert, men like Valjean are incapable of change, consigned for ever to those lives of the criminal world. Redemption and reconciliation are only for those who are obedient to the law. On the other hand, the novel and the musical proclaim the flawed nature of Javert's perspective. Redemption and reconciliation are available for everyone because grace can neither be limited nor confined by law.

The encounter at the end of Fantine's earthly life is a means for expressing and experiencing light through darkness. Consequently, the darkness which threatens Fantine and which surrounds Javert is the reverse of what one would expect. Rather than death-dealing, it is life-giving, a creative, positive darkness, a darkness within which Valjean will not only raise Cosette to the light, but also Fantine as he continues to journey toward it himself.

As Valjean is more and more able to open himself to the Light, he comes into the Light and draws others with him as he was drawn by the bishop. One discovers here a solidarity in salvation as well as in sin. For Valjean, to "raise [Cosette] to the light" is for him to apprehend the Light, to be enlightened by it. The end result is not Hugo tugging at the strings of the reader's heart but Hugo suggesting that Valjean's encounters, no matter with whom, reveal clearly to the attentive reader the kingdom of God's grace rendered unto us as pure gift. The reconciling work of the one man who draws the whole world to himself on the Cross leads to another man's decisions to see his relationship with God as much more than a private affair.

On the stage, Jean Valjean fights with Javert, knocks him out, and escapes. In the novel, at the same point, Javert consigns Valjean to the town lock-up, from which he escapes. After he secures his fortune of six or seven hundred thousand francs, he is re-captured (though Hugo passes over the details) and put aboard the prison ship, Orion. That this is omitted from the musical does not weaken the stage production. However, it is important to note that Valjean's escape from the ship results from his rescue of a man who had lost his balance while setting the main-topsail. Valjean falls into the sea and is presumed dead, but the saving of the seaman's life becomes the occasion for Valjean's freedom. Once more a good deed leads to opportunity, in this case the chance to fulfill his promise to Fantine.

Chapter 6

The Thenardiers: "Masters of Iniquity"

During the early days of the rising popularity of *"Les Miserables,"* Stacy Keach hosted an Arts and Entertainment Network production, *"Les Miserables*: Stage by Stage." In the course of that program, the composers of the musical remarked that in the stage version the Thenardiers are a decidedly different couple from the ones created by Hugo in the novel. On stage, for the sake of relief from the overwhelming gloom of Fantine's shattered dream, life of prostitution, and subsequent death, of Valjean's confession to the court of his real identity, and of Cosette's seemingly hopeless dream of a "castle on a cloud," the Thenardiers function as a source of comic relief rather than as Hugo's indictment of the criminally rapacious element which comprises the hellish culture of the Paris underworld, rather than as an indication of the hell which awaits the ones who pursue money at the expense of everything else, especially their own souls.

However, if one attends carefully to the various images and the mixing of the harsh notes which convey an itchy palm with the jollity of the tavern revelry in those numbers in the musical which focus on Thenardier and his wife ("Master of the House," "Thenardier Waltz," "Dog Eats Dog," and "Beggars at the Feast"), then it becomes apparent that the librettist and the composers have not ignored the demonic for the sake of the comic; rather they reflect accurately the characters created by Hugo in spite of the raucous hilarity on the stage. The final line sung by the Thenardiers in the musical acts as a fit summary for their petty, empty lives as evidenced in the novel and on the stage: "And when we're rich as Croesus,/Jesus, won't we see you all in hell!" Predatory to the end, voracious in their pursuit of the edge, Thenardier and his wife are a travesty of all that is real so that whatever they pursue, whatever they represent, is ultimately either a distortion or a perversion.

When Hugo introduces the reader to the Thenardiers, he notes that they belong to "that indeterminate layer of society" which has neither "the generosity of the worker nor the respectable honesty of the bourgeois" (p. 150). Dwarfish in nature and spirit, monstrous in their single-minded focus on the self, the innkeeper and his wife are incapable of grasping that kind of higher reality embraced by Jean Valjean. They are creatures without hearts, committed totally to that avaricious itch which blinds them to the infinite joy which is designed to be theirs if only they could but choose to behold it. Hugo goes on to inform us that there is never any thought of an about face, moral or otherwise, rather a gradual sinking into the abyss. They choose hell and their descent is not some gentle climb downward begun with some morally ambiguous act, but a headfirst fall, embracing evil at all moments and in all choices, a conscious desire without any hint of conscience to reverse the precipitous drop, to descend into "the bottomless circles of the void." The Thenardiers are of the kind who "always retreat into the shadow, going backwards rather than forwards through life, gaining in deformity with experience, going from bad to worse and sinking into even deeper darkness" (p. 151).

The reader's first encounter with the Thenardiers occurs when the bereft Fantine decides to give Cosette into their care. The focus is dual: the young and destitute mother carrying a child of three and believing naively that God has guided her to the master and his wife, the couple who see in Fantine nothing other than a weak creature who is to be devoured. The nature of their depravity is measured easily after the bargaining for Cosette has been completed. A short time later a neighbor reports to Madame Thenardier that she had just seen a young girl sobbing "as though her heart would break" (p. 150). The response of the master and his wife is heartless; there is no mitigating compassion, only an immersion in the self: they have managed to take care of their own bills; without ever meaning to, they have set, sprung, and closed a trap.

Madame Thenardier, pictured by Hugo as an ogress, a "mountain of sound and flesh," has little capacity for love and expends on Cosette only malice, a malice which is intensified by her apparent tenderness toward Eponine and Azelma. As degenerate and hardened in her way as her husband is in his, she functions as the archetypal evil stepmother and in the musical, true to her archetype, she arouses Cosette from the reverie of "Castle on a Cloud" and sends her into the frightening darkness of the forest in order to fetch some water from the well. All that is left for Cosette is the hope conveyed through the power of her imagination. Immersed in darkness, eclipsed by Eponine and Azelma, the dirty and abused Cosette is terrified of the woods. Her plea—"Please do not send me out alone,/Not in the darkness on my own!"—is rebuffed by her mistress—"Enough of that or I'll forget to be nice! You heard me ask for something and I never ask twice!" Sometimes the audience will chuckle at this, even laugh, perhaps guffaw, but there should be no mistaking the inherent threat in what Madame Thenardier asks. Indeed, she cannot forget to be what she has never been.

Though a child, Hugo argues that Cosette is not alone in her terror: "No man walks alone through this night-time forest without a tremor....Wild shapes haunt the distance, the air we breathe is a black emptiness, we want to look back and are afraid" (p. 350). No wonder that this apocalyptic horror can be repressed only momentarily by the vision of her mother, a "lady all in white," who will tell her that she is loved, before she is brought back to the ugliness of the moment as though her "very soul were becoming merged in darkness" (p. 350).

Acerbic in her treatment of Cosette, Madame Thenardier reminds us of the horrors of psychological and physical brutality which dominate a child's life and imagination when that child is reduced to a mere monetary transaction—"ten rotten francs your mother sends me." This theme of abuse was introduced when Thenardier's letter to Fantine was intercepted, a letter which demanded more money. It is a theme which will be pursued at the bargaining table and in "Thenardier Waltz" as Valjean secures Cosette's release for 1500 francs. The caustic nature of the remarks which Madame Thenardier directs at Cosette are not to suggest that she loves instead Eponine and Azelma, her own daughters, and that Cosette is unfortunately an economic necessity which has intruded on that love. Rather those remarks reveal a woman incapable of love who discovers in Cosette an easier and more fitting target for her vituperative outbursts.

Joy is an impossibility for this shrewish woman, for her daughters only an illusion, and for Cosette a seemingly hopeless dream. To paraphrase Traherne, those who embrace the world endorsed by the Thenardiers will never enjoy the world aright because the sea will neither flow in their veins, neither will the heavens clothe them nor the stars crown them. They will become heirs of hell rather than of the world and then heaven. On the other hand, eventually, through Valjean's mediation, Cosette will discover eventually all the elements of joy and joy itself. Her "castle on a cloud" will later become a reality, but as the ward of the Thenardiers it can never be more than a dream, a vision which the witch and her husband delight in in their attempt to smash. A stench surrounds the monstrous Madame Thenardier, the putrefaction of a demon whose soul rots as she brutalizes Cosette so that the child knows "nothing of the world or of God" and is constantly "nagged at, slapped and punished," a defenseless creature who must have been "a storm of violent and undeserved chastisement" (p. 153). Madame Thenardier and her husband are people of such vulgar mind that they are unwilling, even unable, to discern beauty and choose instead to destroy it.

Unlike Jean Valjean, who discovers painfully who he is and learns to live with that ache so that he grows into a whole man, Thenardier is a chimera, "ready to wear whatever coat the occasion called for" (p. 342). (At the end of the novel, Marius answers Thenardier's question about who Thenardier might be with a summation which penetrates the innkeeper's various identities: "You are also the workman Jondrette, the actor Fabantou, the poet Genflot, the Spaniard Don Alvarez, and the widow Balizard.... And you're a thorough rogue."–p. 1184) A master of disguises and aliases, Thenardier cannot recognize the mortal danger which attends his unrepented crimes. Master, indeed, he controls everything by a "kind of invisible, unwearying magnetism" (p. 343) and is motivated solely by his desire to get rich. Such a craving has replaced any tendency toward morality and thus Thenardier has yielded willingly to the sickness eating at his soul.

So consumed is Thenardier that he isolates himself increasingly from any semblance of a meaningful existence. His emptiness lies in his repeated self-definition as calculating and controlling, a person who first slams the door and then bars it against any kind of moral communion with the world. "What does it matter to you whether he's an imbecile or a philanthropist?" Thenardier asks his wife explicitly with regard to Jean Valjean, but implicitly with regard to anyone. All that matters in the end is that the customer has money and that he can be separated from it.

When Thenardier makes his initial appearance on stage during the frolic of "Master of the House," we discover in his bawdy and jovially furtive movements and in the lyrics a man who is remarkably consistent with the one created by Hugo in the novel. This dramatic consistency is supplemented in the musical by a raucous verbal condemnation which, paradoxically, masks as it reveals and, ironically, issues from the mouths of Thenardier's patrons, who continue to support his establishment every year, and from his own mouth. His own confession is of such an open, boastful, and boisterous nature, one which is so rollicking, that it can camouflage his essentially vicious persona if one does not attend carefully and the masking of his true self is what Thenardier does best.

The drunken customers, his "band of soaks," his "den of dissolutes," his "sons of whores," provide us with our only background information about Thenardier: his reputed presence at Waterloo where he plundered the English dead. That "he made a tidy score from the spoils of war" is thoroughly consistent with Hugo's image of a completely voracious man who "put a little something aside." That something consisted of "purses, watches, gold rings, and silver crosses harvested in the furrows of [Waterloo's] corpse-strewn field" (p. 342). Thenardier is a scoundrel whose capacity for consumption is apparent in his physiognomy.

> Thenardier was a small, skinny, sallow-faced man, bony, angular, and puny, who looked ill but enjoyed excellent health—that was where his deceptiveness began. He smiled constantly as a matter of precaution....He had the sharp stare of a weasel and the general aspect of a man of letters...he was thoroughly crooked, a sanctimonious knave (p. 341).

Indeed, his wife has defined him well – "hypocrite and toady and inebriate"– though she would never dare to brook his rule. Thenardier sacrifices willfully any hint of possible truth to the expediency of the moment. Whatever vocation he might have embraced has been repudiated for the sake of money, and always at the expense of others: the battlefield dead, Fantine, Cosette, Valjean, Marius. He is a man in bondage to avarice and cunning, a slavery which disables him so that his soul is incapable of any movement toward an acceptance of grace.

Early in the novel, we discover that the Bishop of Digne preaches a sermon that condemns the French government which has enacted a law known as the "tax on doors and windows....God gives air to mankind and the law sells it" (p. 29). In the musical, we discover that the nuances of such a system are woven hilariously into the lyrics of the bawdy barroom ditty, which introduces the "master of the house." For the innkeeper, "everything has got a little price." No matter what form the charge takes, it is disguised as the legitimate pricing of services. The goal remains always to relieve his customers of an additional "sou or two." In an ironic parody of Valjean's journey toward the kingdom of God, Thenardier invokes the name of Jesus four times in "Master of the House," each time as an expletive directed toward the fleecing of his customers. For this master, the trick, the deception, lies in the fixing of prices and those prices are increased by watered down wine, stolen money, and altered weight. He will bleed his customers, "skin them to the bone," while harboring contempt for this "sorry little lot," this "dirty bunch of geezers."

His purpose is to use his skill at fixing prices to increase his wealth, to become "rich as Croesus," the king of Lydia who was fabled for his vast riches and reputed misery if anyone were discovered to be wealthier. Yet, indicative of the inherent moral flaws of such a practice and pursuit, Thenardier has neither progressed very far nor have his endeavors amounted to very much. Instead of wealth gained morally and used beneficially, avarice has yielded only a spiritual malaise, an ennui which cannot be separated from the very nature of the path Thenardier has chosen to journey. His is the very opposite of the course chosen by Jean Valjean; Thenardier continues to descend into the pit as Valjean ascends toward the kingdom of God.

That path of cunning is decided upon at the expense of belief in anything other than the self's satisfaction and thus the Thenardiers will never be rescued from their blindness. Their mutual journey toward hell is neither a voyage into some unnamed morality which appears to offer something other than Christian truth nor is it even into immorality. More correctly, they are amoral and thus the journey is into nowhere. When Madame Thenardier defines her husband as a hypocrite, the accuracy of her remark becomes readily apparent in the bargaining for Cosette.

Hugo tells us that "the gulf that nature had created between Valjean and Cosette, the gap of fifty years, was bridged by circumstance. The over riding force of destiny....The man's entry into the life of the child had truly been the coming of God" (p. 392). Aware of his promise to Fantine, he is ready to bear a burden at whatever price and discovers in the process that Cosette will sustain and nurture him as well. But first the exchange must be completed and Valjean knows that in order to help Cosette he must speak the language spoken by the Thenardiers, the language which reduces any exchange to the terms defined by money.

Thenardier's hypocrisy is apparent when, at the beginning of his exchange with Valjean, he states that money doesn't really matter at all, that what he cares about is Cosette. Yet, immediately after he makes this assertion, he turns immediately to his real concern as he speaks "frankly, as between honorable men" (p. 375). Cosette costs money; he and his wife are not rich; he's had to pay for medicine; "Monsieur, I need fifteen hundred francs." Kretzmer captures the moral decay of this couple in his libretto as he has them express, in shrill tones, what a treasure Cosette is: "What to do? What to say? Shall you carry our treasure away? What a gem! What a pearl! Beyond rubies is our little pearl! How can we speak of debt? Let's not haggle for darling Cosette!" Yet haggling is exactly what transpires as if the exchange of Cosette were merely the matter of bartering for flesh in some sort of bazaar. As the stakes rise, as the Thenardiers waltz their way through the transaction to the tune of their own greed, each step is orchestrated carefully in order to profit.

Economic metaphor, especially that of precious jewels, dominates the vocabulary used by the Thenardiers. Cosette is nothing other than a possession and an implicit "mine" punctuates their dialogue with Valjean. Money's terrible power colors everything they do and, unlike Valjean, who lives freely in simplicity bestowing elsewhere his fortune, the Thenardiers are incapable of recognizing that mere accumulation of riches leads to an impoverished spirit. Yet even such a spirit, demonic to its core, can recognize its opposite, a man of great moral strength. Hugo tells us that such perception for the innkeeper "was a matter of intuition; he understood it instantly and finally" (p. 376).

Seizing the moment, Thenardier blurts out his price—1500 francs—and Valjean's response is sardonic in the musical and the novel. "No more words. Here's your price. Fifteen hundred for your SACRIFICE" (emphasis mine), he sings as the bargain is agreed upon and he takes Cosette away from her prison. In the novel, Hugo writes that Valjean is able to regard Thenardier with a degree of contempt and pity which can arise only from a man who can live with paradox, with inner tension: he regards Thenardier "with eyes that seemed to pierce to [the] heart" (p. 376). Valjean perceives quite clearly that the couple are a mixture of what Grossman describes as "sham compassion and superficial sentimentality—a charade of romantic sensitivity" (p. 105). The separation of the voracious couple from the child whom they have abused will be final:

> "Monsieur Thenardier, one does not need a passport to travel five leagues from Paris. If I take Cosette with me that will conclude the matter. You will not be told my name or my dwelling or where she will be. My intention is that she shall never again set eyes on you. I mean to break every connection with her present life. Do you agree to that—yes or no?" (p. 376)

The waltz of the Thenardiers has been completed; a measure of freedom beckons Valjean and Cosette, and the musical refrain of "Castle on a Cloud" suggests that what was once despair with only the hint of a dream now becomes a dream about to be realized.

As Valjean escapes with Fantine, a gap arises between the novel and the musical. Nothing on the stage accounts for the miraculous escapes from Javert, the entrance into Paris, the life in the convent—all the stuff of melodrama—or for the aliases embraced by Thenardier as the mastermind of the Paris underworld, yet the musical manages to conflate the disparate events so that they merge into a unified whole without damaging the thrust of the novel.

When we next encounter Thenardier, this time in the streets of Paris, it will be ten years later. He will be the leader of a gang, but no mention will be made of the Patron-Minette, of what Hugo refers to as that "great cavern of evil" which exists "beneath the social structure" (p. 621), of that "incurable blackness" which gains "possession of the soul [and] becomes Evil" (p. 622). The stage production does not permit a detailed analysis of each member of the gang, though they are named: of the lean and cunning Babet whose eyes are vacant, of Claquesous who is "darkness incarnate," of the urchin turned vagabond turned desperado, the pliant and ferocious Montparnasse.

Unlike the novel, the musical has neither the intent nor the leisure to examine the causes of such deprivation as found in this collection of scoundrels, but it leaves no doubt (in spite of the occasional humor) that such an element exists (and continues to exist), that "ghostlike [these wraiths] return and always the same, only bearing different names and clad in different skins" (p. 626). Thenardier and his cohorts, having plotted the robbery of Valjean, image the epitome of moral decay. It is Javert, the Paris police inspector, who describes with contempt and accuracy the venomous and protean group which Thenardier masterminds: they are "vermin":

> Look upon this fine collection.
> Crawled from underneath a stone.
> This swarm of worms and maggots.

Not fit for communion with society, destined by choice and circumstance for at least hell in this world and, if Thenardier is prophetically on target, the next, their entire design is to pick to the bone the unsuspecting victim, to exist as parasites gorging themselves on a society which they believe exists only to satisfy their appetites. Malicious, subtle, deadly, and furtive, this gang lacks any hint of conscience and is incapable of rising above the level of the brute.

Once again we are made aware of the particular power of money to corrupt. While Valjean has developed a healthy respect for it as a means whereby he uses his fortune to aid the poor and while Marius refuses to compromise his principles in order to have it and thus lives in poverty himself, Thenardier is ensnared totally by the apparent potency of treasure. While money can convey great benefits, he, his wife, and his gang lack the moral courage and spiritual insight to discern any principal other than the self and the self's consuming desire to possess riches, to smell profit in every engagement.

Yet it is much more than just the smell of profit for Thenardier; it is also the justification for that smell. While his guests point out his profit at Waterloo during "Master of the House," in "Dog Eats Dog" he supplies his own condemnation expressed as a justification for the evil he has chosen to do: "Well, someone's got to clean them up my friends before the little harvest (of bodies) disappears into the mud." He is a true denizen of the sewer, a metaphorical "sincerity of filth" which pleases and soothes his vitriolic spirit. Armed with pliers and with the gates of the cloaca outlined above him, the always predatory innkeeper makes his way across the stage stopping only to wrench gold from the teeth of victims who have fallen at the barricades. Thenardier is a sewer rat "among the sewer rats—a breath away from Hell." But some day that breath will expire and hell will be his, that which he has acknowledged and that for which he has longed. Hints of gold, pretty rings, watches—all are the booty which he believes is rightfully his because in his immoral universe God refuses to intervene and for all practical purposes is as dead as the "stiffs at his feet." Yet justice there will be and it will roll down like a river, its righteousness like an inexorable stream, and then Thenardier will face that Face which he believed neglected to take into account the world and those who act in its drama of redemption and salvation or damnation.

The penultimate scene of the musical is a romping reprise of "Master of the House," this time titled "Beggars at the Feast." However, in the midst of the Thenardiers apparent triumph as they exit the stage with stolen silver falling from its hiding place beneath Madame Thenardier's dress and an innocent shrug as if to say "who me?" one becomes aware of some important truths. While by this time in the novel Madame Thenardier is dead, on the stage she joins in the deceptive final utterance: "And when we're rich as Croesus, Jesus won't we see you all in hell!"

The novel gives us the best clue to a moral reading of what happens to Thenardier and, by implication, to his wife. The subtle and serpentine deceiver will escape to America. The full nature of his end remains thus hidden from the reader, but Hugo implies that such amorality will be punished eventually. Thenardier's acts against humanity, his attacks on the integrity of his victims, and his never ending attempts to appropriate for himself what belongs to others will lead ultimately to that hell where he believes he will see everyone else. Mistaken in his belief that life is nothing more than an "easy picking" to be grasped, that moral choice is solely for the decent who are "mostly broke," Thenardier will finally be alone as he is now, immersed in that hell where there is neither exchange nor interchange.

In spite of the jocularity which always marks the Thenardiers on the stage, we ought never to forget the malignancy which lies below the surface, the rapacity which seeks only to consume, to be the dog which eats the other dogs. Deceptive, surreptitious, malignant, Thenardier is more brutish than human, an indication of that world which exists when any bond of common integrity is dissolved. Unloved and unloving, his life is bestial and he is never able to yearn for home. Desiring always some sort of undefined status, embracing forever aliases because he will not name who he is, he will never permit himself to be loved, to be possessed by God. He will choose to ignore the truth that God has fallen in love with him and he will never know what Valjean knows: the truth of Saint Antony's belief that "the whole earth set over against heaven's infinite is scant and poor."

Chapter 7

Javert and the Stars: Order and Chaos

At the end of every Broadway performance of *"Les Miserables,"* the cast of characters makes its appearance at the curtain call. When Javert comes out from the wings and makes his way to the apron of the stage, his appearance is often accompanied by hisses or catcalls as if he were the villain of the piece who has played his part well. A dark figure, certainly; "terrible, but not ignoble" (p. 267), as Hugo writes of him; more accurately a dramatic foil for Jean Valjean rather than villainous or demonic. Certainly one responds to the stern and unyielding character on the stage, the totally committed enforcer of the unyielding penal law, as in the novel, but in this response, valid though it is, I believe that one can miss easily what is at the core of Javert's being: "respect for authority" (p. 274). It is this respect which defines the atmosphere in which he exists and which one can gloss over quickly if one attends neither closely to the musical nor knows the essence of Javert as depicted in the novel.

> It must be borne in mind that the core of Javert's being, the climate in which he lived, the very air he breathed, was respect for authority. He was all of a piece, admitting neither question nor compromise, and in his religious faith, as in all things, he was both superficial and rigidly orthodox. It goes without saying that for him the highest authority was that of the Church. A priest, in his eyes, was a soul incapable of error, a nun a creature incapable of sin. These were souls

> separated from the world by a wall with a single door which
> opened to allow the passage of truth (p. 274).

One never questions Javert's orthodoxy; unassailable, it is even admirable. Instead, it is that his faith, his trust, is "superficial", even shallow, especially in its failure to recognize one of the essential tenets of that faith: that all have sinned and fallen short of the glory of God, even the priest and the nun. Thus it is no wonder that in the novel and in his soliloquy, "Stars," we see a man misguided because he has chosen to conceive of truth as some sort of legal system comprised of axioms and theorems, of mathematical exactitude which can be grasped solely by some higher mind such as his which has surrendered itself entirely to the authority of that system.

Javert's respect for authority arises from an observation and a decision made early in his life: the observation that "there were two classes of men whom society keeps inexorably at arms length — those who prey upon it, and those who protect it" (p. 165), the decision to join the police because he possessed a "profound instinct for correctitude, regularity, and probity, and a consuming hatred for the vagabond order to which he himself belonged" (p. 165). Thus for Javert, only a single moral stance can exist and his life is disciplined in accord with an absolute commitment to that stance. To live in creative tension when confronted with apparent contradiction, such as the redeemed criminal, is not an option for him. The end result is that he becomes a cynic who refuses to trust beyond the narrow confines of what his limited vision can perceive. This is evident in all his dealings with what he perceives to be a criminal element and sometimes his perception is warranted as with Thenardier and his Patron-Minnette, but at other moments it is flawed as with Fantine and Valjean. For Javert, a woman like Fantine possesses no virtue and that Monsieur le Maire should take her side in the affair with Bamatabois is abhorrent to him while "men like [Valjean] can never change," a thrice repeated assertion in the musical, a contention which he believes accurate because his blindness inhibits any deeper insight into the character of an individual. Such a perspective is flawed seriously because it permits for no exercise of love and forgiveness. Such a hardness of heart will destroy what ever opportunity he will have to grasp that vulnerability is a condition of love, that the forgiveness of others is a condition of being forgiven.

The simple principles on which Javert bases his life are "admirable in themselves" (p. 166), but when they are carried to extremes, when they are unseasoned by the theological virtue of love manifesting itself in forgiveness and the possibility of reconciliation and restoration to society, they become "almost evil" (p. 166). A life contained in two words, "wakefulness and watchfulness" (p. 166), is a life of disciplined servitude and while such a discipline is not in itself a bad thing the only kind of obedience and discipline which can lead to liberation is obedience to God, to that light which shines through the veil of the law and which is characterized by perfect love. When obedience is unseasoned by love, then the individual becomes subtly perverse in the delusion that as an absolute protector and enforcer of civil law he is doing God's will. Instead of freedom, Javert is enslaved, imprisoned in the narrow confines of a limited existence, obsessed with the "meaning of the law" and the infliction of that meaning on all who come under his thumb, and, tragically, blind to that light which he believes he embraces and serves. Redemption is out of the realm of possibility for anyone who dares to transgress the literal law and ignore its meaning. Such individuals comprise nothing more than a "swarm of worms and maggots," garbage to be swept away and relegated to the ash heaps of Paris.

In the Prologue of the musical, Javert defines himself in harsh and strident tones which convey his belief in an absolute code, an inflexible system which refuses the intrusion of any kind of prophetic word of love. It is impossible that Fantine or Valjean, or anyone else who has broken the law, should ever change, that women who have given themselves over to prostitution or men once bent on revenge are capable of restoration into a community of love because guilt has been acknowledged and forgiveness accepted. When after his tormented confession at Arras, Valjean confronts Javert in the hospital while at Fantine's bedside, mercy and three days are all that Valjean requires, but the inflexible and unyielding Javert hides behind the safety of certainty in his conviction that the thief will always remain a thief and thus he uses the law as a shield to defend and protect himself from love and forgiveness. He chooses to neglect Christ's command to love and forgive one's enemies, to take seriously "forgive us our sins as we forgive those who sin against us." As C. S. Lewis notes in several places, it is not that someone like Javert (or anyone else) should reduce in himself the "hatred he feels for cruelty and treachery," but that he simultaneously, and almost paradoxically, should hope that such a man "can be cured and made human again" (*Mere Christianity*, p. 106), which is what takes place in Jean Valjean. Secure in his belief that the criminal can never change, he is also secure in his understanding of himself as also incapable of change, and this is what will lead eventually to his suicide. Such hardness of heart destroys ultimately what Alan Jones perceives to be one's "ability to become [an experiment] in vulnerability because, in [his] hardness, [he] believe[s] that there is nothing to forgive" (*Passion for Pilgrimage*, p. 116).

The singing in counterpoint in this number includes a confession from Javert, one that may be missed easily by audience and reader. Though he acknowledges that "every man is born in sin" and that "every man must choose his way," his system of belief does not allow for a sinless redeemer, for the God in Christ who has taken hold of Valjean's life. Javert, "born inside a jail with scum like [Valjean]," has made his choice to serve authority and thus life must fall into a kind of mathematical precision. The only problem is that he cannot see that such exactitude leads to almost a lifeless regularity. So narrow the world he chooses to inhabit, so inflexible the prism through which he perceives all existence, he imagines that such a path is the sole way and thus his life is robbed of a great deal of meaning and his resulting isolation, always feared, frequently respected, but never loved, prevents him from ever discovering his true self. A passion for such objectivity, for clear thought unclouded by the whimsy of feeling no matter how valid the subjective emotion at a given moment, is a good thing, but when that passion is so narrow in its perspective that it isolates the individual from the love that can be known and which is often apparent it begins to feed on itself and, in doing so, begins to destroy that self.

In the chapter "The honesty of Javert," the inspector, who has often been harsh in his life, confesses that he has "treated others harshly" and that "it was right that [he] should do so" (p. 200). This integrity is apparent in his confrontation with Monsieur le Maire when the mayor testifies on Fantine's behalf and requires that he should scourge himself if he is willing to scourge others. Hence, he tenders his resignation and while the offer is admirable it is evident that he is blind to the compassion and mercy which stands before him in the person of Jean Valjean, a Jean Valjean he could not imagine if he but knew that the mayor was the convict who had broken his parole. For a man to embrace exclusively only one way of knowing, to affirm solely a single minded pursuit, is to admit fear without acknowledging or even being aware of the admission. It is to refuse the kind of knowing which Valjean offers, an understanding which is a model of compassion and insight, forgiveness and love. Thus monsieur le Maire, tutored by the bishop and aware totally and terrifyingly of the danger which Javert threatens as chief inspector, is able to decline to accept Javert's resignation. On the other hand, because the growing clarity of vision which characterizes Valjean is foreign to him, Javert cannot recognize holiness and cannot perceive the activity of God in the life of Valjean. Javert becomes the symbol of the "everyman" born blind from birth who chooses to refuse to have his eyes opened by the light of love.

When Javert looks at the stars and reaches for them as he sings as if to grasp what they represent, they become for him a metaphor for precision and order. In his perception of them as "sentinels,/ Silent and sure./Keeping watch in the night/Keeping watch in the night," we discover his attempt to ascertain the will of God by induction from the order which God manifests in nature. The stars shine; they radiate light; they "[fill] the darkness/With order and light." However, Javert is content with that secondary light and shows no inclination to trace its source. His proclamation that his way is God's way indicates his belief that he is an heir to a tradition which is rooted in Judeo-Christian practice. Yet he repudiates inadvertently the one who is the Light of the world, becomes obsessed with his duty to the law, and thus misses the real truth which emanates from the stars: that the garbage which he seeks to clear from the street can function as a special revelation in Christ, in this case mediated through the Bishop of Digne to Valjean and through Valjean to Javert. When one chooses to be blind to such a revelation because it contradicts apparently all the tenets of one's existence, then wrath takes over and one such as Javert will never rest until the quarry can be found and placed safe behind bars. As someone once noted, such anger, such an obsession, is the inevitable consequence of a rejection of God's love rendered even more hideous when the one who rejects such love believes that he has embraced it, that his way is "the way of the Lord," whereas Valjean's is a "way in the dark."

While Jean Valjean journeys ever so slowly and painfully toward Calvary and into the mystery of redemptive love, Javert seeks to complete his journey accompanied only by knowledge as possession, as certitude, and thus he can never know the mystery, can never enter into its heart and apprehend its redemptive power. Javert never abandons his claim to his belief that the law is doctrinally absolute: "And so it has been and so it is written/ On the doorway to paradise/That those who falter/And those who fall/Must pay/The price." As H. A. Williams notes in *True Resurrection*, Javert's weakness lies in his trust "in his accumulated mental constructs [which he has mistaken] for reality" (p. 94). His consuming desire to have Valjean "safe behind bars," his refusal to rest until such is the case, mark him as a man whose vision is distorted and thus as one whose pursuit of the truth must essentially be warped.

A wonderful irony exists in Javert's apostrophe to God: "Lord, let me find him." It is uttered as a prayer and the prayer is answered. He finds Valjean often enough, but because the prayer is vitriolic in tone and is offered by a man whose vision is flawed, he cannot ascertain the answer. Javert is unable to surrender himself to the God who reveals himself in Valjean and the reason for this is that Javert does not comprehend what he needs in order to be set free from bondage. Valjean is able to confess this need, to sing openly "forgive me all my trespasses and take me to your glory," but Javert's imprisonment is so great, so complete, that he cannot conceive of it in such terms. Finally, when he can begin to recognize his need to be free, he cannot embrace that need. Having yielded to the law all his life, Javert has been engaged unknowingly in a kind of suicide which, ironically, becomes a preparation for an actual suicide. His way is not the way of the Lord; he knows the law, but he does not know grace.

His perception of Valjean as a fugitive on the run, "fallen from grace," is only partially correct. That fall has taken place in Valjean's theft of the loaf of bread, the repeated attempts at escape, and the coin stolen from Petit Gervais which breaks the conditions of his parole, and will continue to manifest itself because Valjean is a sinner, but for him the redemptive work of God in Christ has become a personal reality. It has taken hold of his being and become concrete in such a way that every misstep is accompanied by acts of contrition, but "Stars" makes it evident that Javert has not embraced grace in the same manner. As one can behold at first the beginning and then the consummation of glory in Valjean, that glory forever lies dormant in Javert. Javert is so busy proclaiming his doctrine that he will not and cannot hear what Valjean has said, and if he cannot hear Valjean, he will be unable to hear God.

Saint John of the Cross wrote in *The Dark Night of the Soul* that the soul "must empty itself of self in order to be filled with God" and, to paraphrase Sir Thomas Browne, if we cannot empty ourselves of self, then, when God comes, He will find no room for himself because we are too full with ourselves. Part of the nature of Javert's sin is that he places himself at the center and thus the demand for humility which self-abnegation demands, the renunciation of pride, becomes impossible. His existence becomes an obsession with the law he serves, so much so that he becomes a kind of zealot, one whose entire focus is on the domination and destruction of another's soul. While his desire to embrace principle remains forever admirable, such a desire is distorted and disfigured ultimately so that he will be unable to be rescued from the depths of his imprisonment. The music he sings, the tune by which he attempts to orchestrate his life, is so discordant, almost shouted rather than sung, that it becomes apparent to all but himself that he has become overly confident in his own wisdom and thus he can never fathom the grace which surrounds Valjean.

Javert's two great numbers on stage are solos, consistent with his misguided belief that it is somehow good to be alone, but such a belief must be ultimately an illusion, a symbol of spiritual emptiness. Man is made for communion with other men; it is in such exchange that he discovers joy and love. Yet when one denies relationship, when one tries to keep at arms length all the realities which give existence its meaning and depth—love, joy, forgiveness, faith, hope, selflessness, exchange—whatever he believes, no matter how apparently noble or principled, must be a misconception of what is righteous. Javert turns justice into an obsession – "I will never rest" – and this religion of law and judgment is a belief in the supremacy of the hunter over the hunted.

In the novel, Valjean and Javert encounter each other by chance though neither is at first certain of the other's identity. Once that unknown in the equation is solved, Javert senses a thrill known only to "the mother who recovers her child and the tiger who recovers his prey" (p. 422). In the musical, a similar encounter takes place when Javert unknowingly rescues Valjean and Cosette from Thenardier and his band and then discovers, courtesy of the innkeeper, that the man he has just aided had a brand upon his chest. The discovery prompts a reflection in terms of two questions – "Could he be the man I hunted?/Could it be he's Jean Valjean?" – followed by a decision – "Let the old man keep on running./I will run him off his feet" – which leads to the soliloquy, "Stars." The certainty inherent in the solo mirrors the portrait of Javert at a comparable moment in the novel.

Then, with a demonic and sensual pleasure, he settled down to enjoy himself. He *played* his man knowing that he had him, deliberately postponing the climax, granting him a last illusion of freedom, relishing the situation like a spider with a fly buzzing in its web or a cat letting a mouse run between its paws—the ecstasy of watching those last struggles! (p. 423)

Here one discovers the supreme arrogance which arrives only with the certitude that the power which one wields is based on authority: "Mine is the way of the Lord." For Javert at this moment, it is never a possibility that his principles are flawed or in error.

In his huntsman's pursuit of his prey, in his rejection of love, compassion, and mercy, Javert's solo becomes a chorus of noes. Again, he cannot see clearly how the stars provide coherence when there could be chaos, "filling the darkness with order and light," and thus it will be he who "must pay the price" because he must eventually "falter" rather than Valjean. As Grossman notes in a penetrating comment, "we see that [Javert] speaks for society and yet lacks access to personal sentiments. The whole of nature—including the very stars in heaven—seems implicated in the process, the fullness of the outside compensating for the emptiness of the inside" (p. 106). Javert's life, devoid of love, is lived out under the illusion that it is nevertheless ordered, fulfilled, and complete. Such a deception has the power first to twist and then wreck the best engagements that a man may be offered by virtue of its single-minded and blind desire. The failure to know love can cost one his life and no matter how dedicated that life is it is essentially sterile, cold, and lifeless.

The divine light breaks forth forever into the world in a multitude of forms and whether that light is manifested in the natural world of the stars or in the human world in people like Jean Valjean, it becomes incumbent upon us to learn to behold that light so that it may inform and direct us. Because Javert cannot see that it is by light alone that he exists—though he thinks he does—he refuses to acknowledge it when it shines more brightly in the person of Valjean. The consequence is that for him, and for any who embrace existence as he does, life will shrink and wither as one refuses steadfastly to wrestle with and engage the true light which challenges the presuppositions which lead to the absolute creed embraced or adopted by men like Javert.

Chapter 8

The Revolutionary Spirit:
The ABC Society and Love as Friendship

In the opening of *"Les Miserables,"* the Bishop of Digne sings to Jean Valjean "see in this some higher plan." In effect, he dares Valjean to begin to view his life and the world around him with newly opened eyes, with eyes cleansed by the love of God and mediated through the selflessness of the bishop (though the bishop would never have expressed it or seen it thus). Once Valjean chooses to respond to that challenge, Hugo tells us that a change takes place which can be described only as a transfiguration. The key, however, is that this dramatic alteration in the soul of Valjean is not held on to as some sort of private deposit; rather, it spreads like ripples in a pool and calls to account silently all those with whom he comes in contact. For the most part, in neither the musical nor the novel are these responses to the newly transfigured Valjean elaborated upon, with two notable exceptions: Fauchlevant and Javert. Fauchelevant, rescued by Valjean from under the wheel of a cart, returns the favor within the confines of Le Petit-Picpus, the convent which provides Valjean with a respite from Javert. On the other hand, in Javert, we discover what transpires when one refuses adamantly to see with cleansed vision, to behold what changes God can bring about in an individual, or, having seen, determines not to reconcile what is true with his own flawed perception of reality.

I think that something similar, at least metaphorically, transpires in the novel and the musical with regard to the ABC society. Functioning as a political plot which parallels the soteriological one which focuses on Jean Valjean's journey toward freedom and redemption, the revolutionaries who comprise the ABC, and who are led by Enjolras, seek to demand that the microcosm, which is Paris and her miserables, open its eyes to a vision of Utopian harmony and peace, to that liberty, equality, and fraternity which were the hallmark of the revolution of 1789, but which had been eclipsed. While the musical neglects to familiarize the audience with the background for revolution (it is often assumed that the historical moment is 1789)—though "Red and Black" and "Do You Hear the People Sing" suggest adequately that freedom is at the heart of the movement—and omits entirely Hugo's view of history and politics expressed in the lengthy and discursive chapter on Waterloo and the acts and pronouncements of Marius' uncle, Monsieur Guillenormand, we are reminded in both novel and musical that the young men had "a religion in common: Progress" (p. 564), that the moment has arrived for all "to decide who [they] are," to choose what is "the price [they] might pay." As Enjolras says in the novel, "It's just as well to know where one stands and whom one can count on" (p. 735). The existence of the ABC derives its essence from "the pure blood of principle coursing through its veins" and its young adherents stand for "uncompromising right and absolute duty," the "underground portrayal of the ideal" (p. 564).

What matters most here is "principle." No matter one's politics, then or now, the key element is that these politics be guided by principle and Enjolras' leadership is an attempt to help his comrades grasp a vision which lies in his mind as one of awe and wonder. Professor Grossman comments pertinently about this in a footnote when she writes that Enjolras "echoes the ideas of Pierre Leroux, the utopian socialist thinker" who defined "his vision of the ideal future through the concepts of humanity (what links each individual to past, present, and future generations), solidarity (the equivalent of Christian charity, that is, of love for one's fellow human beings), and perfectibility (the possibility of moral and social progress)" (p. 132). The utopian vision is a nice dream—the word in Greek means no place—this side of paradise, but neither Hugo nor the librettist ever lead us to believe that Eden is a possibility in this life.

Enjolras' rhetoric is most often a stirring call to the renewal of the political order because for him such renewal lies at the core of one's existence. Simultaneously a scholar and a warrior, "a soldier of democracy in the short term and at the same time a priest of the ideal rising above the contemporary movement" (p. 557), Enjolras attempts to compel his revolutionary friends to see beyond personal interest and grasp the ideal which he nourishes in his soul, a vision of life in which people will not be slaves, in which the people will free themselves from the shackles of an oppressive regime which refuses them even enough bread much less the possibility of a night at the opera.

The British pub, the dormitory common room of the American university, the French cafe, these are the places where issues are raised and the dreamed of ideal is championed, where Courfeyrac can crumple a charter and toss it on the fire. Hugo has it right when he describes such a gathering.

> This was the tone of the gathering, sarcasm, jest, and foolery, the thing that the French call wit and the English call humor, good taste and bad taste, good reasoning and bad, the tumult of talk volleyed from every corner of the room to echo like a cheerful cannonade above the talkers' heads. (p. 577)

However, to gather and converse, no matter how noble the cause, can never be enough. The tide of ideas flows, but the moment arises when the "rich young boys" must decide whether what they are about is merely a game or whether the issues are sufficient that they dwarf other interests. Is the plight of the hungry, the destitute, and the outcast merely to be rhapsodized about as glasses are lifted to a cause? Or is engagement to be affirmed so that the people can be set free from the paralysis which marks France's spirit? The two songs which Enjolras leads suggest vividly the latter.

To release people from a paralysis which suffocates is an admirable goal, but one which must not be approached as mere revolution. This is often missed in the musical and one is tempted to think that revolution of any kind becomes a justified and legitimate option. Hugo takes pains to tell us often in the novel that this is not to be the case and perhaps nowhere is he more concise in drawing distinctions than in Part IV, Book Ten, ii, "The root of the question."

> The sound of righteousness in movement is clearly recognizable, and it does not always come from the tumult of an over-excited mob. There are insane outbursts of rage just as there are flawed bells: not all tocsins sound the true note. The clash of passion and ignorance is different from the shock of progress. Rise up by all means, but do so in order to grow. Show me which way you are going; true insurrection can only go forward. All other uprisings are evil. Every violent step backwards is mutiny, and to retreat is to do injury to the human cause. Insurrection is the furious assertion of truth, and the sparks struck by its flung paving stones are righteous sparks. But the stones flung in mutiny stir up nothing but mud. Danton versus Louis XVI was insurrection, but Hebert versus Danton was mutiny.
>
> Thus it is that if, as Lafayette said, insurrection is the most sacred of duties, sporadic revolt may be the most disastrous of blunders.
>
> "Sometimes insurrection is resurrection." (p. 887)

The students engage in "insurrection" with passion and, idealistic though they may be, they apprehend a truth which those they seek to serve and set free cannot yet grasp: that the "faint revolutionary stir" is like a "rising tide complicated by a thousand eddies" (p. 555) or, in Kretzmer's paraphrase, that the "river" of ideas is "on the run" like "the flowing of the tide." Charged with clarity of vision, they seek the "furious assertion of truth" (p. 887), a truth which falls on deaf ears because the people lack the passion necessary to complement the movement. The danger is that such inertia on the part of the populace will result in a waste of energy and lives on the part of the ABC, a burning out which will leave behind only ashes. But for Hugo, "Today's Utopia," flawed though it may be, "is the flesh and blood of tomorrow" (p. 555), of a place beyond the barricades where the world once longed for does indeed exist.

The revolutionaries acknowledge a spirit of freedom and their cry attempts to pierce a world which has chosen to ignore the lives of the people to the point that the people themselves have become deaf. The juxtaposed colors, red and black, become a metaphor for those who ignore or miss the signs of the times, a stirring attempt to remind that the "colour of the world is changing day by day," that those who ignore the signs place themselves in a precarious state. What Enjolras advocates is the belief that history is a stage on which the people play out their roles and, dead or alive, contribute to the final chapter, the one which lies ultimately beyond the barricades and which, paradoxically, is merely the preface or first chapter to that story which is paradise and which goes on forever. The world about to dawn is the world in which freedom is the dominant chord being struck. Thinkers are free to pursue their thought and "religious believers [are] all equal before the law" (p. 1004). If heaven itself is indeed "the one religion," then what matters most is playing well one's role in the drama of salvation.

The higher goal toward which Enjolras strives and into which he seeks to draw others parallels the struggle of Jean Valjean who, under the auspices of a higher good, makes his own pilgrimage to the barricades and beyond. Self-sacrifice in the name of an ideal becomes an example for individuals and nations as the "higher call" takes precedence over all else. Enjolras' vision is that of a "splendid new dawn breaking through the clouds on the horizon" (p. 737) so that the lives of those who join in the crusade don't count in the larger framework when measured against the ideal. A powerful contrast is provided by Marius whose passion is suddenly for a woman and whose belief is that a world empty of her is incomplete and can yield only despair.

In the midst of the red-black rhetoric sweeping across the stage in song, Gavroche announces that General Lemarque is dead. Hugo gives us only a few paragraphs on Lemarque, but they are sufficient to illustrate why his death becomes the rallying cry for the ABC. He was a man of "action and high repute" (p. 892), courageous in battle and dispute, eloquent, the staunch upholder of the cause of liberty, the people's man who refuses to ignore the hungry and thirsty, the stranger and the naked, the sick and the prisoner. In some respects, he is the Bishop of Digne in the political arena. In his belief that the death of Lemarque will "kindle a flame," Enjolras breaks into "Do You Hear the People Sing?", a song of expectation which is as rousing in its own context as Henry's Saint Crispin's Day Speech at Agincourt or the strains of the 1812 Overture. The symbols and the music speak to us more powerfully than words alone because they transcend explanation, because, perhaps, they cannot be understood solely by the mind at all. In their idealism and naivete, the ABC offers its souls and bodies to freedom and equality in anticipation of an age to come. An irony exists in the immediate offer because the people do not join in either the song or the dream, but even that irony dissolves in the final affirmation that there does exist a world beyond the barricades which men long to see.

Someone wrote that "we who are about to die demand a miracle." For Hugo, that miracle is the recognition that the best way to live is to die every night, to undergo, as does Valjean, a transfiguration. In that case, in the musical the militaristic "Do You Hear the People Sing" becomes a kind of prayer proclaimed by those who will join the chorus of a new dawn which will sweep across the "meadows of France" now watered by the blood of the martyrs. While Enjolras knows that death is likely, to die is not his design. He sees himself and those who join with him as the instruments of God and, to paraphrase Tertullian, he believes that their blood will be the seed of a new life of freedom. The blood of these witnesses reflects the conflict and the cruelty alive in the world, a blood which can be understood ultimately only in light of the death of the one on the cross.

However, as always, a price is to be exacted beyond the rhetoric and the music which leads to the charge. The glory of enlistment leads to the qualms which exist before the battle, to the wistful, despairing, and balladic "Drink with Me" after the first success. In the novel, the members of the ABC gather as "though this were the most peaceful of student occasions" (p. 935) and recite love poems.

> The time and place, the youthful recollections, the first stars showing in the sky, the funereal quiet of those deserted streets and the inexorable approach of desperate adventure, all this lent a touching pathos to the verses.... (p. 935)

The "shrine of friendship" binds each to a cause and to each other and in such a bond one discovers a nobility and pride, a sublime strength in the defiance of death and the acceptance of fate. Here exists passion for fellowship, for a mutuality which is heightened and intensified by a steadfast loyalty. As C. S. Lewis notes in *The Four Loves*, "Two friends delight to be joined by a third, and three by a fourth, if only the newcomer is qualified to become a real friend. They can say, as the blessed souls say in Dante, 'Here comes one who will augment our loves'" (p. 92).

Hugo is correct when he argues that such an insurrection must fail because practical resources are limited, because ammunition is short and one dead man cannot be replaced. By contrast, repression knows no such constraints, has no conscience with regard to the number of men expended, and operates with no need to spare bullets. Still, there is hope, an "unless": "So these battles of one against a hundred must always end in the crushing of the rebels UNLESS (capitals mine) the spirit of revolution, spontaneously arising, casts its flaming sword into the balance" (p. 1022).

In the final chorus of the musical, one is left with the hope that the people do indeed desire to climb to the light, that they "will live again in freedom in the garden of the Lord." A universal uprising can occur so that the prodigious light of God shines through the chaotic darkness of a fallen world and then the distant dreams will be a reality and will usher in the future, the kingdom of God.

The ABC functions as a kind of prophetic body, a massed passionate idealism whose heartbeat conveys a sense of immediacy which needs to be quickened and intensified. Yet, inevitably, before the prophet can be heeded, death must occur and in *Les Miserables* all the revolutionaries who remain at the barricade die, with the exception of Marius. But the dead do not die; they retain a solidity unlike anything one may experience in this world. As Eliot writes in *Four Quartets,*

> The communication
> Of the dead is tongued with fire beyond the language of the living.
> Here, the intersection of the timeless moment
> Is England and nowhere. Never and always.

Much like Valjean when he remembers his fellow prisoners, Marius recalls death with all his senses tuned: he hears Gavroche "singing amid the musket fire," he feels his lips touch Eponine, "the figure of all his friends appear to him and then vanish" (p. 1125). A grief which pierces the heart may occur when one discovers that he has outlived those friends beside whom he fought and with whom he laughed, next to whom, at "a table in the corner" of a tavern, he could, in the idealism of youth, "see a world reborn" and where he joined to light a flame. Such a loss cannot be grasped unless one comprehends that Marius has been deprived not only of their physical and immediate presence but also of those intangibles which they were able to draw from him. As Lewis notes, such an individual needs other lights than his own "to show all his facets" (*The Four Loves*, p. 92). Yes, says Hugo, in response to Marius' unspoken question, these young men had really existed, but even in their deaths the light of their idealized principles, the light which is themselves and their utopian dream, the light which owes its brightness to the One who is the true light of the world, refuses to be extinguished.

The musical enhances the poignancy of this moment as Marius is alone on the stage, seated at a table, recovering from his wounds. As in the novel, he sees only from within and imperfectly what the audience sees before it as the phantom faces and phantom shadows take on a momentary solidity and provide a moment of mystical communion with the transcendent. Because the ABC, corporately and individually, is alive in his memory and in his imagination, and alive on the stage to us, Marius' words engage us with the realities of existence, with what one poet calls "a timeless, tribeless circumstance," and thus keep the song from mere sentimentality. The truth that the supernatural has access to us and we to it is affirmed.

Within the structure of the ABC, Hugo embraces a view of friendship consistent with that of the ancients, a perspective which sees the posture of friends as standing side by side, the logic of Enjolras complemented by the philosophy of Combeferre, while Jean Prouvaire, Feuilly, Courfeyrac, Joly, Bossuet, Grantaire, and Marius add their own balance. In their deaths and in Marius' song, we discover what Allchin defines as a "gathering together of men of all kinds, of every human circumstance, a detailed enumeration of all those for whom [Marius] felt bound to pray and give thanks" (*Living Presence*, p. 59). The spirit of insurrection can reach out and touch eternity and no matter how the figures from his immediate past threaten to fill Marius' mind with darkness and a sense of impending disaster, no matter how what was sacrificial appears to have been a "last communion" at dawn at a "lonely barricade," they do signal a new tomorrow and offer us the opportunity to stand against repression and poverty, to join in the crusade, to embrace the dream that for the "wretched of the earth there is a flame that never dies."

At the end of Part III of *The Lexus and the Olive Tree*, Thomas Friedman shares a secret with the reader: the wretched of the earth do **not** (bold mine) want to journey to the barricades or beyond; instead, they want "to go to Disney World. They want the Magic Kingdom, not *"Les Miserables"* (*The Lexus and the Olive Tree*, p. 364). In the globalized world of today, such an assertion may appear to be true, but what Friedman and so many others miss is that both Hugo's novel and the Broadway musical give the lie not to the facts of the assertion but to the philosophy which lies behind it and which continues to promulgate it. Novel and musical recognize implicitly that the mere yearning for economic success and even apparent fulfillment of such a dream is never enough, is only an illusion which God in his mercy must shatter. *Les Miserables* proclaims unabashedly that we are not meant for this world, that what lies beyond the barricades is our true home, the place where the "chain will be broken and all men will have their reward," the place where many mansions exist waiting to be filled and where joy is offered beyond anything imagined here.

Chapter 9

Eros Reborn:
Marius and Cosette

One of the difficulties encountered when a sprawling literary epic is brought to the stage is that of compression: how does one meld or fuse disparate elements into a single theme within a limited time. In the musical version of Hugo's work, this difficulty occurs not only as one attempts to merge the ABC with the main plot, but also with the integration of the romantic element which surfaces between Marius and Cosette. Happily, the musical does not attempt anything approaching the lengthy meetings between the young lovers detailed in the novel. Rather, it encapsulates the essential ideas which Hugo articulates about love and weaves them into a series of melodies which reflect accurately what is for Marius a Beatrician vision, a moment of grace, of hope, of desire – "to be struck to the bone in a moment of breathless delight" – so that whatever one's focus has been previously, it has been shifted to a new ideal, even if she exists at first only as a ghost, only as a phantom springing from a mind which is open to love.

Before Marius engages Cosette, before he is smitten completely and enraptured, the new being which is taking shape within him is essentially philosophical and is fostered solely by thoughts of his father and his country. He is not politically astute and his agenda shifts as he becomes aware of his heritage, but underneath everything is the ideal of France's rise, the dawning of a new age. Penurious at this point in his life after a falling out with his grandfather, Marius is quite unaware of his good looks and, in spite of the flirtatious attention paid to him by Eponine, has "no girl of his own for the simple reason that he ran away from them all. Thus he continued to live in solitude" (p. 603). Courfeyrac even offers good natured advice and urges him to give the girls a chance. Marius' response is to "avoid women more strenuously than ever, both young and old" (p. 604). However, Marius had been accustomed to taking strolls in the Luxembourg garden and had noticed there an elderly man and a young girl, the latter "skinny to the point of ugliness, awkward and insignificant, although her eyes promised to be beautiful; but she gazed about her with a kind of unheeding assurance that he found displeasing" (p. 604). For a year he takes no interest at all in the girl and then changes his itinerary for six months so that he does not encounter her.

Yet when he next sees her, she has undergone a radical transformation. The dirty, hapless Cosette of the Thenardiers and "Castle on a Cloud" has become a "tall and beautiful creature, endowed with all the charms and graces of womanhood at the precise moment when these are still mingled with the innocence of childhood, a moment of fragile purity only to be conveyed by the words, 'fifteen years old'" (p. 605), the "despair of painters and the delight of poets" (p. 606). I quote this at length because we do not see quite the same transformation on the stage. When Marius bumps into her, it is quite by accident, but the chance encounter produces the same reaction. The vision which Marius has is pure gift, the flame which ignites the wood, the spark which sets on fire a world which for him had only been latent. Hugo is lyrical about this and suggests repeatedly that if we know anything of love, of the joy of eros as opposed to the mere carnality of Venus, then it is axiomatic that one such as Marius can be lost immediately in the throes of love and henceforth think only in terms of romance.

> The first gaze of a spirit that does not yet know itself is like the first glow of sunrise, the awakening of something radiant but still veiled. Nothing can convey the perilous charm of that unexpected gleam, shedding a sudden, hesitant light on present innocence and future passion. It is a kind of

unresolved tenderness, chance-disclosed and expectant; a snare laid unwittingly by innocence, which captures a heart without intending or knowing what it does, a maid with the sudden gaze of a woman. (p. 607)

A key here is that the trap laid is done so "unwittingly" and by "innocence." It is not the maneuvering of one with predetermined designs, not the feline stalking of prey. It is quite contrary to what transpires between Fantine and Tholomyes. For Tholomyes, Fantine is a purely external diversion, someone whose person matters not. She exists to provide merely some sort of excitement, to enhance the thrill of the romantic episode. Fantine's transgression, born of what she believes to be love, is ultimately a surrender to the purely sensual desires of Tholomyes. On the other hand, the "purity and ardor" of the relationship between Marius and Cosette displays the power of innocent love to "implant in another heart" (p. 607) the joyful desire to respond. While at this point we do not know what will become of them, there is no hint of that boredom which engulfs Tholomyes and his friends and leads them always to other beautiful women. While Tholomyes and his cronies look always to the external pleasures provided by a woman, while Hugo suggests that they will seek always newer and newer variety, an infinite increase in pleasure, for Marius the treasure will remain always right beside him.

After initial contact in the musical, Marius asks Eponine "That girl! Who can she be?" Eponine, having already recognized Cosette, hears the exclamation in Marius' remark. Such immediate reaction cannot be lost when another supplants the one who would be loved. The man might not know that he is so transparent, but the woman will not miss the signs. Cosette may have been a "bourgeois two-a-penny thing" only six months ago, but now she is the possessor of that beauty which is "at once feminine and angelic" (p. 611), which "had once moved Petrarch to song and brought Dante to his knees" (pp. 611-612).

It is no wonder that when he joins his friends, they are aware immediately that Marius has undergone a dramatic alteration in temperament. Late for the meeting, Joly remarks on his pale complexion, as if he had encountered a ghost, but Marius identifies immediately the cause: *she* was like a ghost only because she disappeared so suddenly. The musical does not have the leisure to draw out Marius' deepening involvement, his bumbling trips to the Luxembourg, but it does not need to. These men, these comrades in arms and philosophy who raise their glasses in toast to the pretty girls who have gone to their beds, know all too well that what has happened to Marius is serious: "Marius was in the first violent and entranced throes of a grand passion. A single look had done it" (p. 612). And Marius' lovesickness on the stage is captured perfectly in Grantaire's cynicism, which corresponds accurately with Hugo's description in the novel.

For Grantaire, Marius is not so much an object of ridicule or scorn as he is one of naive innocence who would be better cast in a light and romantic opera featuring a "Don Juan" than as an integral part of the ABC.

> "Marius in love!" cried Grantaire. I can imagine Marius in a fog, and he has found himself a mist. He belongs to the tribe of poets, which is as good as saying that he is crazy. Marius and his Marie or Maria or Mariette, whatever she's called, they must be a rum pair of lovers. I can guess what it's like—rarefied ecstasies with kisses all forgotten, chastity on earth and couplings in the infinite. Two sensitive spirits sleeping together amid the stars." (p. 924)

"Rarefied ecstasies" is precisely what their love is and while it cannot be detailed so in the musical the sense of purity and innocence, wonder and awe, is never lost. However sexuality exists for the others, for Marius it is pure gift from above though never articulated as quite this at its inception. For them, love is, as C. S. Lewis notes, charged explosively with a character which can only be described as holy, an awesome and dynamic thing, as a joy which is invested with permanence and thus as a joy which elicits a willingness on the part of the lover to invest himself totally in the beloved.

In the midst of Enjolras' rousing rhetoric about "battles to be won" so that the new world which is about to arise will put to rest the "dark of ages past", Marius turns the colors red and black inside out and they become metaphors for desire and despair, for the nature of the soul in love rather than part of a political agenda. When Enjolras sings, the atmosphere is charged with the electricity of the ideal cause, whereas Marius' inverted response has to it a more wistful quality. In the former, there is an implicit challenge to discovery, to the need to arrive at a decision which will color the destiny of France; in the latter, the use of "had" implies a condition which Marius believes only he can fathom and his images are comprised of the delight of love, breathless, turning the world upside down, confusing what had once seemed so clear. A chance meeting is the catalyst which sets love in motion, but such an encounter is only the title page of the story which will be told as the journey into deeper love and freedom unfolds.

Enjolras' response is that of the urgency of a higher call whereas Marius imagines that he can get by on love. Without denying the validity of Enjolras' vision, Hugo acknowledges that Marius is right, that love is sufficient, but Hugo is also quick to imply that such love shrivels and dies in the absence of contemplation and adoration. The merely human love, which is often only romance or the passion of the moment, needs to be transfigured, transcended, if it is to be grounded securely and true to its deepest self, as Alan Jones points out in *Journey Into Christ*, (p. 95). His soul on fire, Marius' love is so directed toward Cosette throughout their meetings that it, to once more cite C. S. Lewis in *The Four Loves*, "gazes and holds its breath and is silent, rejoices that such a wonder should exist" (p. 33). His love for her brings to him a quality of life which is shrouded in mystery, which he has never known, and which contains a sense of the marvelous, and it promises to give him what Diogenes Allen refers to as "utter bliss" (*Love*, p. 118).

The glory of the love which exists between Marius and Cosette, the power of their falling in love, of their mutual innocence and purity which will neither be invaded nor breached, lies in their ability to behold in each other that which doesn't give in order to get. No motives exist to cheapen the attraction, only the discovery of joy in the mere act of giving itself. For Cosette this is imaged in her feelings that somehow, mysteriously, her life has begun at last for she has neither knowledge nor experience of such eros. I think that Kretzmer captures this when he has her sing that times exist when she catches in "the silence of a faraway song" which sings of "a world that [she longs] to see" just "out of reach" but waiting for her. Something almost indefinable exists in this strange love which has been given birth and yet escapes the heart and mind of the innocent Cosette. The "faraway song" is like a Siren which calls to the listener to embrace something which for the moment is unknown and can be only a hint of joy. It is a longing, an intense desire which suggests that satisfaction is beyond the things of this world, but it is also a longing which must remain only a promise until her love finds her.

That hint begins to take shape in the Rue Plumet when Cosette wonders whether people can "really fall in love so fast." The coming of love changes a hesitant, diffident person into someone who is radiant, alive with an energy which seems to arrive on the wings of a prayer as she begins to wonder about her life, a life which takes on new dimensions now that she has left the convent. This phase of her development is omitted from the musical, merely suggested in the questions and answers that somehow don't integrate properly. While Valjean leaves the convent with her because he believes that to insure his own happiness at the expense of a child would be an egregious error, would be "to do outrage to a human being and tell a lie to God" (p. 758), might even lead Cosette to hate him, she is intrigued by her unknown past, especially the small valise which Valjean always keeps in his possession (p. 759).

While Cosette wrestles with a passion which she has not yet begun to comprehend and with a past which remains elusive, a mystery, Marius has been overcome, even besotted, drunk with delight. In the novel, his newly discovered love develops over several years, but, in its own way, it is as explosive and lightning quick as on the stage. Hugo tells us that summer and autumn passed and winter came and Valjean and Cosette had not set foot in the Luxembourg. Marius' sole thought is "to see that enchanting face again" (p. 637); his focus has been re-directed, so much so that "he had ceased to be the hot-headed dreamer of dreams, the bold challenger of fate, the youthful builder of futures, his mind teeming with castles in the air" (p. 627). Love which burst "like the music of angels, the light of the sun" is light and such light causes life to stop by virtue of its presence, whether in physical immediacy or imaginative longing.

In "A Heart Full of Love," one is immersed in a duet which is suffused in images of light, in paradoxes of being simultaneously lost and found. It is a duet grounded in mutuality – Marius and Cosette are totally entranced in such a way that even their gazes trouble so that "each sustained the same hurt and the same good" (p. 773). For them, the purity of their love becomes an introduction into a way of knowing which is a mystery, which is to receive a mystery. Their response to each other is that of adoring love, of a posture of adoration which becomes like worship because it is the selfless outpouring of each to the other. Hugo expresses it thus:

> Cosette in her solitude, like Marius in his, was ready to be set alight. Fate, with its mysterious and inexorable patience, was slowly bringing together these two beings charged, like thunder-clouds, with electricity, with the latent forces of passion, and destined to meet and mingle in a look as clouds do in a lightning-flash.
>
> So much has been made in love stories of the power of a glance that we have ended by undervaluing it. We scarcely dare say in these days that two persons fell in love because their eyes met. Yet that is how one falls in love and in no other way. What remains is simply what remains, and it comes later. Nothing is more real than the shock two beings sustain when that spark flies between them. (p. 773)

Love has been uncovered and it comes to the lovers as a form of grace, as a free and unmerited gift. What they feel for each other as expressed in "A Heart Full of Love" is a product of who they are and thus the need never exists to create or increase artificially the intensity of their passion. As Allen remarks about such a need, to do so would be an attempt to absorb the other, to "pressure a person to surrender his or her individuality" (*Love*, p. 18).

The reality of the glance, its power to administer the shock, is not only a fact of falling in love, but also the initial step in what the young seek, even though all do not understand when they have found it. The encounter, the engagement, the first surge of mutual delight between Marius and Cosette is a microcosm of what is. In the musical motifs, the recurrent theme of hearts filled with love, what Marius and Cosette see must be re-spoken, re-imaged because there is no other way in which the as yet unborn images can begin to take shape. In their songs, we catch something of the sound of the human heart as it expresses (or tries to express) the joy and pain which lie at the center of love. As Diogenes Allen is correct to point out, herein, even subconsciously, each is able to recognize the other's reality, a necessary component not only of romance but also of friendship (**Love**, p. 18).

Initially, love breaks out like light so that the dawning of a new awareness is both an end and a beginning--"And my life seems to stop as if something is over and something has scarcely begun." It produces a heightened consciousness and perception as it changes the way in which all else is perceived, as it moves the one in love from darkness into light, out of the shadows into a new and more encompassing reality. In that sense, "A Heart Full of Love" becomes a lyrical meditation, an exchange between a Dante and a Beatrice, a "vita nuova" of its own. We are not meant to be alone and the love between Marius and Cosette functions in such a way that their private thoughts, emotions, and experiences are intertwined with what Grossman sees as the "workings of the entire universe" (p. 110). This observation is substantiated by Hugo in his brief and lyrical chapter on love when he remarks that love is "the reduction of the universe to the compass of a single being until it reaches God" (p. 803).

Marius and Cosette convey the essential mystery which binds together lovers as part of the dance and each note in Hugo's musical composition on love is a variation on the single principle that love transforms and transfigures and that the common denominator in all love is God: "that which love begins can be completed only by God" (p. 805). Agape, divine love, God's selfless love for his creation, poured out without limit, this is what raises eros to the level of wonder and awe. That Marius and Cosette transcend time and space through the purity of their imaginations is an occasion for joy because it is part of their pursuit of the way of chastity and thus consistent with their escape from the slavery of a lustful and self-destructive way of life. Within two such souls dwells what Hugo calls the "divine spark" (p. 804), that "fiery particle that dwells in us, immortal and infinite, which nothing can confirm and nothing extinguish" (p. 804).

Marius is absorbed totally with beholding Cosette so that he never makes the mistake of attempting to acquire or retain her. The integrity of his vision permits him to feel and be filled with something which approaches adoration and rapture. It is the kind of clarity of sight championed by Herbert in "The Elixir," Muir in "*The Transfiguration*," and Lewis in "Meditation in a Toolshed": all express a power to behold, to discern; all proclaim that wonder and awe are available and accessible to those who choose to open their eyes and behold.

In the neo-pagan, post-modern, sexually liberated anything goes world of the late twentieth century and the new millennium, the purity of Marius and Cosette's love is not only refreshing but also Edenic, a taste of what was meant to be but which had been lost. It is no accident that the lovers meet in a garden; Hugo intends it as a microcosm of paradise and they respond in such a way that they will not be the ones to spoil what is a gift from above.

> During that month of May in the year 1832, in that wild garden with its dense tangle of undergrowth that grew daily more impenetrable and richly scented, two beings composed wholly of chastity and innocence, bathed in all the felicities under Heaven, nearer to the angels than to men, pure, truthful, intoxicated, and enraptured, shone for each other in the gloom. To Cosette it seemed that Marius wore a crown, and to Marius Cosette bore a halo. They touched and gazed, held hands and clung together; but there was a

gulf that they did not seek to cross, not because they feared it but because they ignored it. To Marius the purity of Cosette was a barrier, and to Cosette his steadfast self-restraint was a safeguard. The first kiss they had exchanged was also the last. (pp. 844-845)

Thomas Howard has remarked that Charles Williams's characters seem able to find glory in a mud puddle. So, too, with Hugo's lovers who in their love are able to behold what is hidden in each other and bring it to light. Hugo again: "They existed in that state of ravishment which may be termed the enchantment of one soul by another, the ineffable first encounter of two virgin spirits in an idyllic world" (p. 845). The imaginative lover has the power to transform what he beholds into an even higher expression of truth so that in the purity of his adoration he hears a music which those less tuned cannot apprehend, perhaps the "melody of the spheres" (p. 846). Because purity and restraint function as a barrier and a safeguard, mutual obligation and respect are present from the start since self-indulgence and mere sensuality are never an option. Such implicit mutual resolve suggests Marius and Cosette's determination "to meet the whole range of life together" (*Love*, p. 78).

One of the problems which Hugo and the musical must overcome is that Marius and Cosette risk the possibility of becoming essentially static figures dwarfed by the giant presences of Jean Valjean and Javert. However, I don't think that either work permits this to occur. In their love, in their reveries, idyllic almost, they are preserved in the holiness of their engagement and thus are never reduced to some sort of cardboard non-existence. In the sanctity of their love, they begin to know each other in a way that would have been impossible had they merely given free reign to latent appetites. For Marius, such love is real because it is unthreatened and uncontaminated by negotiable assets. For Cosette, those assets are never considered and thus she remains free from any possibility of mercenary corruption. Freed in this way, they are able to make the most of their moments of perception. Marius pours out his whole being toward Cosette and in consequence discovers a deepening stillness which distinguishes his love from that of his friends and his grandfather. His pursuit of the ideal and his willing commitment to a self-imposed discipline set him apart from and in opposition to that world view which has the use of others as its god and the exercise of power as its principal order.

While Marius and Cosette may never emerge as quite so lively a couple as Austen's Darcy and Elizabeth, they will be far from static, more a Bingley and Jane who enjoy a quiet and shared life. As Allen points out, such a relationship will have a strength and durability that will never be able to be reduced to mere pleasant feelings which arrive one day and depart the next (*Love,* p. 79) They will grow in wonder and delight at the vast context of God's action. The words they sing may be old, but still they ring true and by the end of the novel and the musical, even in their flawed responses to Jean Valjean, they retain constancy in their love which promises growth and offers hope. Part of the eternal present which unites the living and the dead, they will be sustained by what Allen expresses in a wonderful metaphor as the great tidal wave of God's oncoming Kingdom and thus unfold more of themselves as they truly come to know each other (*Love,* p. 77).

While the love between the two remains essentially romantic and idealistic, their marriage has within it that seed which will enable their love to achieve fruition: "to love well, always, and faithfully" (*Love,* p. 67). In an observation for which Marius and Cosette function as a paradigm, Diogenes Allen believes that love such as theirs, since it began as disciplined commitment rather than as sensual surrender, it is not a stretch to imagine that this couple, though losing youthful charm as we all must, will retain that intrinsic beauty which God's love bestows freely to each stage of life. Marius will never be a sly old Guillinormand chasing the maids into the bedroom as he bestows upon them the favor of a sensual look, but it does not mean that he will be unable to gaze lovingly at Cosette, or she at him (*Love,* p. 80).

Chapter 10

The Never-Ending Road to Calvary

As has been noted at several points, one of the major themes of *Les Miserables* is that of the journey, the need for any individual to arrive at the awareness that Tabor and Calvary, the glory and the pain, the Transfiguration and the Crucifixion are woven inextricably into the fabric of every human life. One of the more difficult tasks faced by the producers of the musical is how to weave together the various journeys undertaken in a 1200 page novel and conflate them in such a way that they merge at a single moment on the stage and retain their individual integrities while acknowledging at the same time that in that web of glory which is a fact of creation all identities are connected, the one to the other. The solution is set forth in the rousing choral spectacular, "One Day More," which functions as the close of Act I and in which every character defines himself in terms of a particular stage in his journey. The entire number is sung in multiple counterpoints and each character is joined by the common thread of Jean Valjean's opening lines "One day more!/Another day, another destiny./This never-ending road to Calvary" and the choral affirmation which concludes the number, "Tomorrow we'll discover what our God in Heaven has in store."

While all journeys begin at birth, some of the stages along the way become what Conrad's Marlowe calls "illustrations of life, symbols of existence." For Jean Valjean, the beginning of that stage lies in the meal at the home of the bishop because it is in the aftermath of that meal that he begins to open his heart and mind to the good news of the gospel, to commence seeing his entire life as a journey toward redemption and salvation in terms of the Cross. As the bishop honors God in his refusal to ignore his creation as it presents itself to him in the poor, the oppressed, the wretched, and the prisoner, so will Valjean do likewise as he embraces humility and service and seeks to renounce whatever spiritual forces and sinful desires exist which will draw him from the love of God. Because he chooses to travel the road to Calvary, because he refuses to deny what that road offers, he embraces the Cross and undermines that Hell which seeks to drag him into the abyss, which sought Fantine, which will claim Javert.

When Valjean turned himself in to the court at Arras, he had every reason to believe that such a decision marked his Calvary. He even wished that the dreadful cup might pass from his lips, but he chose to be obedient to God's will and engage the suffering which was at hand. However, in his case, the journey to the Cross had only just begun and he needed to continue to discover that in every instance of his "never-ending road to Calvary" the Cross accomplishes everything and that his life is a pilgrimage into the heart of the mystery of the Cross. As he once before wrestled with that tempest within himself which was his conscience, he is again gripped by sadness, so much so that he often cannot sleep and sits for hours with his head in his hands.

The musical can only hint at moments at Valjean's dilemma, especially with regard to his past and Cosette's future. As far as she is concerned, he believes that what has happened is "better unheard, better unsaid." He torments himself as his thoughts return despairingly "to the convent, that sheltered Eden, with its neglected blossoms and imprisoned virgins, where all scents and aspirations rose straight to Heaven" (p. 778) and he longs for that "Paradise from which he had voluntarily exiled himself" (p. 778). But Paradise is not here and not yet for him and we begin to see his life and all its tempestuous torment as a microcosm of the world "silhouetted against the Passion of Christ." Easter is always the taste of the reality which beckons, but one must not rush past Calvary in order to get there. At this point, his thought is of Cosette's preservation and his and so he will leave Paris and go to England. Warned by Eponine, his decision to escape from Javert and the shadows which pursue him is a decisive stage in his journey, one which recapitulates in his mind the itinerary that has defined his life and focuses not only on his agony but also, implicitly, on his movement toward death and resurrection.

As the drama of his redemption unfolds, one can imagine Valjean's arrival at some sort of terminus, a moment at which he decides to become inert spiritually and thus cut short his journey toward Calvary. It could have occurred with Champmathieu, or while he was in the convent, or when he decided to leave France with Cosette. However, such is the nature of his conversion, of his attempt to turn to God once-for-all, that he refuses such choices and his spiritual re-birth recurs constantly within him. For "one more day," endlessly, he wills himself to traverse that labyrinth which appears to be his life, engage the demons which lie within and without, unseen and seen. Professor Grossman expresses it thus: "Repeatedly torn between duty and pleasure, sacrifice and contentment, action and passivity, the hero enacts the moral struggle of 'civilization' itself. In a century replete with man-made horrors, *Les Miserables* continues to disturb and engage us by querying the limits of personal and collective progress with undiminished urgency" (p. 13). Someone once noted that the best way to read Dante's *Divine Comedy* would be to begin with the *Paradiso*. However, like Dante the pilgrim, before we can rest in Heaven, we must first choose to journey through that seemingly spiritual wasteland which is the dark wood. This is the path which Valjean chooses as he enacts "the moral struggles of 'civilization' itself" and begins to enter truly and creatively into what Alan Jones defines as "those twin mysteries of meaning and death" (*Journey Into Christ*, p. 26).

In the Finale of the musical, Valjean will sing "forgive me all my trespasses and take me to your glory" while in the novel he affirms Christ in the crucifix and acknowledges the presence of his confessor, the bishop. This will be discussed in depth in the final chapter. What matters here is the realization that Valjean's journey into the heart of darkness is a kind of crucifixion which must precede the prayer "take me now to thy care" and the light of the resurrection. He will peer into that darkness, even embrace it, because hope also resides there, because, as Neuhaus writes, "the worst word is not the last word" (*Death on a Friday Afternoon*, p. 109). The road to Calvary which never ends remains that costly path to discipleship for those who seek to follow the risen burden-bearer of creation. The motif "one day more" and its variations parallel in their own way Donne's question "What if this present were the world's last night?" As the sonnet implies and as it is echoed by C. S. Lewis in his essay, "The World's Last Night," for anyone and for Jean Valjean in this novel, pain and sin, suffering and torment are the working out "of the free drama of [his] life in the given theater of this world." For Valjean, the journey terrifies and threatens always the possibility of meaninglessness, the menace of the loss of intimacy, and the inevitability of death.

In the simultaneity of a political insurrection, a love affair between Cosette and Marius, the steadfast pursuit by Inspector Javert, and the all-consuming avarice of the Thenardiers which threatens to reveal him at any moment, Hugo tells us that Jean Valjean sees the security of his world begin to crumble. He has become much more cautious, perhaps because of his desire for solitude, and goes out seldom with Cosette. When he does venture out, he goes in disguise and thus Thenardier fails to recognize him on one occasion. Thenardier has become for Jean Valjean "the embodiment of all the dangers that threatened him" (p. 876) while Paris, in its unsettled state, posed an additional danger: "for anyone with something to hide the present political unrest had the disadvantage that the police had become more than usually obtrusive, and might, in their search for agitators, light upon someone like Jean Valjean" (p. 876). While his initial impulse and immediate decision is to escape to safety, he will decide finally to face with courage the loss of all that is familiar and secure. Such is the nature of the road to Calvary, of the process of discovery which arrives at the awareness that it is the Cross which binds together all humanity. In *Centuries of Meditations*, Thomas Traherne wrote the following:

The Cross

is the
abyss
of wonders,
The center of desire,
The school of virtues,
The house of wisdom,
The throne of love,
the theatre
of joys
and the
place of
sorrows;
it is the
root of
happiness
and the
gate of
heaven.

Through such a meditation, one discovers, as does Jean Valjean in *Les Miserables*, that the gift given and the giver are one.

In "The treacherous blotter," a brief chapter at the end of Part IV, Hugo asks a series of questions which return the reader once again to that tempest which seems always to exist within that human skull which is Jean Valjean's.

What is the turmoil in a city compared with that of the human heart? Man the individual is a deeper being than man in the mass. Jean Valjean, at that moment, was in a state of appalling shock, with all his worst terrors realized. Like Paris itself he was trembling on the verge of a revolution that was both formidable and deep-seated. A few hours had sufficed to bring it about. His destiny and his conscience were both suddenly plunged in a shadow. It might be said

of him, as of Paris, that within him two principles were at
war. The angel of light was about to grapple with the angel
of darkness on the bridge over the abyss. Which would
overthrow the other? Which would gain the day? (p. 970)

What is again apparent here is that Jean Valjean's journey to
Calvary is always a journey into himself during which he will
become himself as fully and completely as possible. It is forever
evident that such growth as his depends on one's willingness to
expose one's life to those conditions which are harsh and raw,
threatening always to lacerate and scar the body, the mind, and
the spirit. To borrow a baptismal metaphor, such a choice is not
a sprinkling, a mere dabbling, but a total immersion in a process
which is never completed, a complete commitment to a life
which will surrender itself to being re-made. The turmoil within
the heart, the grappling between light and dark over the abyss
expresses a point made by Alan Ecclestone in *Yes to God*. Valjean's
life, now lived as best he can as prayer at any moment, cannot be
viewed as a journey which notes merely the passing of successive
milestones. Rather it must be perceived as one "in which [he sets]
out once again from [his] departure point with greater knowledge
of the joy and pain involved" (p. 7). It is this continued birth of
awareness which grasps the fact that the road to Calvary and the
Cross is always an affirmation that God cares and is involved with
Valjean in all his life. As Adam and Neuhaus note so convincingly,
the place where Christ has not been does not exist. The road to
Calvary is the road to the Cross and "the Cross is the way to glory"
(*Border Lands*, p. 177), the place where Jean Valjean "might live to
his glory" (*Death on a Friday Afternoon*, p. 183).

To the one so inclined, every new stage of the journey presents
infinite possibilities of joy and pain which need to be embraced.
"One day more," sung in the solitude of his own musings and in the
simultaneity of all that transpires around him, becomes a painful
movement toward personal integrity. This is especially true with
regard to Cosette, a movement which seems slow but which breaks
upon him with tremendous force when he articulates openly what
had been apparent tacitly for a long time.

Jean Valjean, for his part, had a sense of profound, indefinable unease. For some time he had been apprehensively watching this growing radiance of Cosette's beauty, a bright dawn to others but to himself a dawn of ill-omen. She had been beautiful for a long time without realizing it; but he had known it from the first, and the glow which enveloped her represented a threat in his possessive eyes. He saw it as a portent of change in their life together, a life so happy that any change could only be for the worse. He was a man who had endured all the forms of suffering and was still bleeding from the wounds inflicted upon him by life. He had been almost a villain and had become almost a saint; and after being chained with prison irons he was still fettered with a chain that was scarcely less onerous although invisible, that of his prison record. The law had never lost its claim on him. It might at any moment lay hands on him and drag him out of his honourable obscurity into the glare of public infamy. He accepted this, bore no resentment, wished all men well and asked nothing of Providence, of mankind or society or of the law, except one thing—that Cosette should love him.

That Cosette should continue to love him! That God would not prevent her child's heart from being and remaining wholly his! To be loved by Cosette was enough; it was rest and solace, the healing of all wounds, the only recompense and guerdon that he craved. It was all he wanted. Had any man asked him if he wished to be better off he would have answered, "No." Had God offered him Heaven itself he would have said, "I should be the loser." (p. 770)

His consuming desire that "Cosette should love him" functions as a kind of intimation of hope in the midst of what appears as hopeless for Valjean. It is a suggestion that his journey has a destination, but alongside exists the threat that such beauty could be terrible, the "portent of something new" (p. 771). As it has happened so often and sometimes so painfully slowly, the journey must embrace the realization that in order for him to become fully what he was meant to be he must die in order to live. To paraphrase Austin Farrar, in the midst of agony and inner turmoil, he must continue to exchange what most certainly appears to be a living death for Christ's dying life.

When one grasps the fundamental truth which lies behind the image in the grain of wheat which must fall into the ground and die in order to produce other grain, then life becomes a series of fresh beginnings. The "never-ending road to Calvary" is never-ending precisely because one does not arrive until death. And yet, almost miraculously, and sometimes without giving voice to it so completely has one died to self, as with the bishop, the journey is undertaken within the presence of that mystery which is God and which journeys with one. As Alan Jones notes in *Journey Into Christ*, that Valjean begins each day, again and again, one more day, means that he need never despair because he moves, "in Christ, from glory to glory, from what is less real to what is more real" (p. 136). For Jean Valjean, it is not so much that he lays hold of this blazing truth in some intellectual manner as it is that this truth lays hold of him. What he becomes during the course of his pilgrimage to the Cross is not the consequence of those things which he has done but of those things done in him. Valjean becomes a sign post, missed by Javert, that one is always considerably more than he thinks he is, that one's true identity will be always hidden from those whose sight is marred or flawed.

When Jean Valjean first meets the bishop, he is a nearly broken man bent on theft, even murder, and certainly revenge against a world which has rejected him. The journey toward Calvary and the Cross appears to be neither a literal nor a metaphorical possibility since he has never been awakened to the intolerable gospel of love. But once Charles Myriel enters his life, his journey is altered and the restoration and redemption of a once hopeless man begins. Such a moment becomes the catalyst for the flow of God's grace into a man who has been wounded severely by a hostile world and thus healing takes place and re-birth commences. Valjean moves inexorably and affirmatively, no matter the pain and cleansing involved, toward the discovery of what his God in Heaven has in store. In that journey, he will be able to affirm truly that Javert "is wrong and always has been wrong," that he is "a man no worse than any man." The one more day which will eventually be the day of his death will find restored in him the true image of the divine, the Valjean he was always meant to be, the man who has dared the fires of purgation and emerged a person transfigured by the glory of God.

It is dramatically appropriate that Valjean introduce the image of the Cross in "One Day More" because it is the supreme icon of Christ, the magnet which seeks to draw to itself lost mankind, the tree against which the responses of all the other characters will be judged. On Calvary, darkness appears to triumph, but the drama does not end on that Friday afternoon and resurrection becomes a present experience, the journey of the magi of the world toward death and re-birth. As in Eliot's "The Journey of the Magi," Valjean undergoes hardships. It is not quite so easy to follow merely the star over Bethlehem; rather, the voices of temptation arise frequently to whisper or shout that the entire pilgrimage is a folly and even as one draws closer to that which is his means of redemption less hopeful signs continue to appear which may cause the traveler to stray. It becomes impossible to live at ease "in the old dispensation," but the reminder is always there that in spite of the new path to which one clings doubt will arise which will force one to question the validity of the choice, spiritual agony and perplexity will intrude just when one believes that all has been sorted out. No matter. We discover with Valjean that the narrative of history gathered together in the Cross of Christ is the spiritual reality of every individual's life. Valjean is not merely a penitent on the road to redemption and salvation, but all mankind from the Fall to Calvary and the empty tomb. This discovery involves a long and painful process and in *Les Miserables* it is made by a single man at particular moments in his life. Yet, it is also our discovery if we will have it so. As Eliot writes in "Little Gidding" at the end of *Four Quartets,*

> We shall not cease from exploration
> And the end of all our exploring
> Will be to arrive where we started
> And know the place for the first time.

The discovery is that the end is the beginning, that the end is not an exit but an entrance, that the pilgrimage is undertaken for the sake of love and toward wholeness (*Journey Into Christ*, p. 2), and that the dance is real and one is a partner in it.

"One Day More" is not only Valjean's journey though his is Hugo's primary focus. Alongside is the political journey undertaken by the student led ABC in its bid to achieve unity and peace through the "barricades of freedom," the romantic triangle of Marius, Cosette, and Eponine as each attempts to grapple with all the perturbations of love, the first two united by fidelity and mutual innocence, the third longing for love and yet doomed to be on her own, the tortured path of revenge chosen by Javert, determined to destroy the revolution and capture the man whom he has hunted, and the Thenardiers, the parasites for whom judgment is irrelevant as long as they can line their pockets with what the dead leave behind. Pain and suffering are not Valjean's alone. Each enters the world of all the characters and those who have no sense of engagement outside themselves, whether nobly misguided like Javert or completely avaricious and amoral like the Thenardiers, will never discover their true selves or grow into their full stature. For Javert especially, as we will see, the world will always disclose more questions than answers and he will be unable to live creatively with tension and with the fact that Calvary redeems the lost if only they will accept the offer.

All the variations of Jean Valjean's "One day more" function so that the events and problems of individual lives hammer away at the consciousness of the audience. The motif enters into the urgency of each character. It is difficult to capture such simultaneity on the stage, but the counterpoint culminating in a chorus manages it well. While the expanse of the novel provides greater leisure in the unfolding of individual lives and the events surrounding them, Hugo provides the impetus for "One Day More" in his observation that "all these incidents, here slowly related in succession, occurred almost simultaneously in separate parts of the town amid a vast tumult, like a string of lightning flashes in a single clap of thunder" (p. 898).

When Valjean begins the musical number with his observation about Calvary and "another day, another destiny," Marius and Cosette are together affirming their love for each other, but aware of the immanence of separation and the attendant threat. The crown which is his and the halo which is hers will be wrenched away so that these two whose world has just begun will have the promise of the melody they sing in expectation of joy torn from them so that only doubt and shadow remain. For Marius at this point, life without Cosette can lead only to despair and chaos. Hugo tells us that for him to live without her is impossible, that "since she had left him, he could only die" (p. 949). The musical cannot develop the flaws in his reasoning, especially his absurd belief that "she no longer loved him, since she had gone off in this fashion without a word of warning, without a letter, although she knew his address" (p. 949), but their separation on stage allows him to join with Eponine and embrace what he believes to be the life of his father, "braving the musket balls, baring his breast to the bayonets, shedding his blood seeking out the enemy and finding death if need be" (p. 948).

Consequently, Marius asks a series of questions which lead to an internal conflict and the decision to fight at the barricades. When love invades Marius' life in the person of Cosette, his resolve changes. Such is the nature of his love and his youthfulness that he is really undisciplined in terms of his journey. Whereas Valjean has discovered and continues to discover that his pilgrimage is not merely for its own sake, but for the purpose of bearing reality, a reality always shaped and defined by the light of the Cross, Marius' decision to fight at the barricades is born of despair and in response to what had "sounded to him like the voice of Fate" (p. 943). Valjean learns to bear reality in all its fullness while Marius leaves the garden behind in the novel, separates from Cosette on the stage, and goes off to fight with his friends: "Half-crazed with grief, with nothing clear or settled in his mind, unable to face the realities of life after those two intoxicated months of youthfulness and love, overwhelmed by the bewilderment of despair, his only thought was to put a rapid end to his misery" (p. 943).

When Kretzmer has the students sing "One day to a new beginning, raise the flag of freedom high," he echoes accurately Hugo's belief that a revolution consists of "everything and nothing, a spring slowly released, a fire suddenly breaking out, force operating at random, a passing breeze. The breeze stirs heads that think and minds that dream, spirits that suffer, passions that smoulder, wrongs crying out to be righted, and carries them away" (p. 883). For Enjolras and his followers, Calvary does not quite enter the equation with mathematical precision, but its presence is implied in its willingness to journey through pain to glory in the company of others. The students attempt to utter a profound Yes and that affirmation made now in the context of their vision and dream is the preface to that fulfillment which awaits them beyond the barricades when they will have put away the sword.

That one's journey is a "never-ending road to Calvary" is arrived at by Jean Valjean in terms of that self-surrender which must precede self-fulfillment. Whereas his surrender is always to God in the silent awareness that he enjoys a solidarity with those who have gone before him and prepared for death to self and living to God, to resurrection, the surrender made by the students is to a cause. However, as noted earlier, their cause is an insurrection rather than a revolution and "sometimes insurrection is resurrection." While he wishes that so much that has happened to him hadn't, Valjean never renounces his life. By owning the Cross in all its agony, he aligns himself with Calvary as well as with the empty tomb, with all suffering and with the power of resurrection which flows from it. Whereas his journey to Calvary is one of self-sacrifice in the expression of love for the bishop, for Fantine, for Cosette, even for Marius, above all for God, the road travelled by Enjolras and the ABC is sacrificial in the name of an ideal, a principle, an inspiration, which lays hold with extraordinary and mysterious powers and leads at last to that heaven where ultimate freedom reigns.

When the curtain falls on Act I, the Thenardiers remain inflexible in their pursuit of the edge, in their predatory capacity to consume, and Javert is as stalwart as ever in his adherence to order and law, ready to infiltrate the revolutionaries and quell the insurrection. However, all the characters join in an affirmation that any journey is the movement toward the discovery of "what our God in Heaven has in store." The rest of the novel and the musical is the working out of that discovery, but at this point it is Valjean who has become most aware that any journey is not a static condition but a free response to the tree planted on Calvary.

In his solitude, whether in prison or before his trip to Arras, whether in le Petit Picpus or the Rue de Plumet, Valjean discovers in the depths of his aloneness the resources for what he must do, a series of decisions wrought out of inner spiritual struggle. He moves toward an awareness that his life is gauged by a different measuring stick, that length of years or accumulated possessions or power do not matter, but that love given and received is what renews and that love has its origin in God. When Hugo writes of this, it is not that Valjean has grasped it rationally; rather it is and continues to be a mystery into which he has chosen to enter. God has found him, laid hold of him, even seized him, and all subsequent fellowship, or relationship is rooted in that primary relationship, in the decision to take up his cross and walk its way on the "never-ending road to Calvary."

As the curtain falls, the characters sing in unison that "Tomorrow we'll discover what our God in Heaven has in store." For the Thenardiers, it will be death for her and exile for him, a further descent into the abyss; for Javert, an inability to live with paradox and creative tension, a suicide of body and soul; for Eponine, death and redemption as she gives her life for another; for Enjolras and the ABC, death at the barricades, but resurrection in that world which lies beyond them. All the principals are seen in a new light and each subsequent moment brings with it a new awareness, a sense of discovery, and, for some, a progress in holiness to and in God as one moves toward the Kingdom. For Valjean, the movement is even deeper, the journey even more profound because what he comes to know in the struggle is God's love in the shape of personal communion. Such knowledge encompasses all else and this explains how, in the midst of emotional and spiritual pain and suffering, he is able to re-gather his forces, his resources, so that the love which exists in God in Christ accompanies him in the most tenuous circumstances.

The "never-ending road to Calvary" is a journey to the City of God and Valjean's final prayer, "forgive me all my trespasses and take me to your glory," signals that glory is exactly what one is meant for. As C. S. Lewis notes in his essay, "Man or Rabbit," we "shall bleed and squeal as the handful of fur comes out; and then, surprisingly, we shall find underneath it all a thing we have never yet imagined: a real Man, an ageless God, a son of God, strong, radiant, wise, beautiful and drenched in joy" ("Man or Rabbit" in *God in the Dock*, p. 112). This is what lies ahead for Valjean. The Lord of Love once lifted on a tree has drawn Valjean to him, just as he promised he would, and though only a quite unadorned stone will mark Valjean's grave, Hugo leaves no doubt that this pilgrim who has embraced the journey to the Cross will be "drenched in joy."

Chapter 11

Eponine and Gavroche:
The Plight of the Rejected

In a source I cannot recall, someone remarked that he reads in order to place his heart and mind in a wider world of feeling, experience, and thought. And C. S. Lewis notes in his essay *De Audiendis Poetis* that reading is a kind of travelling in the course of which you begin "to see the foreign country as it looks, not to the tourist, but to its inhabitants" (*Studies in Medieval and Renaissance Literature*, p. 2). Then one realizes that the foreign country is also the landscape of one's inner self, that the jealous Othello, the proud Nostromo, the naive Dorothea Brooke belong not merely to post-medieval Venice, a fictional nineteenth century South American state, or mid-nineteenth century England. The country is our country and we are the characters; we are David being pointed to by Nathan the prophet and hearing the accusation, "You are the man!" As H. A. Williams argues so convincingly in *True Resurrection*, it is true that most of us will not be redeemed felons like Jean Valjean, or self-righteous enforcers of the law like Javert, or revolutionary activists like Enjolras, "at least not in terms of our conscious selves and our social personnae" (p. 89). Such observations are not only true of the major characters we meet in a work, but also of those lesser figures, especially when they are portrayed in the depth accorded them by Hugo.

It is tempting to perceive Gavroche and Eponine as somewhat cardboard figures invented to assist the revolutionary and romantic plots, but this would be to miss the point made by Hugo in the novel that to have created Gavroche and Eponine is to have known "the heat of the furnace and the light of the dawn" (p. 495). It is also to fail to notice that on the stage each of them sings of who they are and what they know so that even their notes of failure and despair have a place in our attention. In a very real sense, they are Paris and childhood, and the reader-audience is invited to participate in them from the inside rather than to relegate them to the role of plot devices.

When Hugo introduces the street urchin in "Paris in Microcosm," the first chapter of Part III, "Marius," he notes that such a child is "the dwarf born of a giantess" (p. 495). Little do we know that this is literally and figuratively true, that Gavroche is every urchin as well as the son of the Thenardiers. When Gavroche appears before us on the stage, he fits Hugo's description, "aged between seven and thirteen" and wearing "a pair of his father's old trousers which come down to his heels, and an old hat which belongs to some other father which comes down below his ears, a single brace with a yellow border" (p. 495). This is the boy who in the musical rushes on the stage with alacrity and a hearty "Ow do you do? My name's Gavroche. These are my people. Here's my patch" and invites us not only into communion with him but also with "the beggars at [our] feet" while in the novel Hugo is the artist who attempts to open our eyes to what Ecclestone identifies as the "truth of neglected things" (p. 46). Among others, Gavroche becomes not just a character but a moment out of history and in all history who conveys exactly what has gone dead in the microcosm which is Paris, in the "slums of Saint Michel" where the whores give the "pox" to their customers "till they end up in a box." As Hugo observes, "the 'gamin' stands for Paris, and Paris stands for the world. Paris is a sum total, the ceiling of the human race. The prodigious city is the epitome of dead and living manners and customs. To observe Paris is to review the whole course of history, filling the gaps with sky and stars" (p. 505).

When Gavroche sings "Think you're poor, think you're free, follow me! Follow me!" he invites us, as we have been invited earlier, to open our eyes to a new possibility of seeing. As in numerous other instances, to behold Gavroche is "to look down the throat of time" and to note that the sweeping generalizations of the street urchin have now been particularized in one child, a boy "aged eleven or twelve" who has "the laughter of the years on his lips" but only "darkness and emptiness in his heart" (p. 509). When he bursts on the stage with energy and an apparent joie de vivre, the tendency exists to ignore his essential darkness. Yet he remains part of the chorus of the wretched, those who have "neither hearth nor home, nor any regular source of food" (p. 509) and, ironically, is somehow happy "because he was free." Hugo adds the following:

> By the time the poor have grown to man's estate they have nearly always been caught in the wheels of the social order and become shaped to its requirements; but while they are children their smallness saves them, they can escape through the smallest crevice. (pp. 509-510)

When Hugo introduces the Paris urchin, he uses a series of parallelisms not unlike those used by Dickens in *A Tale of two Cities* and *Hard Times* in order to emphasize dramatically the plight of the street urchin. The repetitive "he has" (pp. 495-496) and the use of the present tense convey the essence of an eternal condition, "born of the rankest clay, but a handful of mud and a breath created by Adam" (p. 498).

These urchins, these "little bands of children" made concrete in Gavroche, add certainly to the text a degree of humor, but one must not forget that though delightful they are also heart-breaking, "at once a national emblem and a disease. A disease that must be cured. How? By light. Light that makes whole. Light that enlightens" (p. 505). And the only light that enlightens thus is the light of God in Jesus Christ, himself the Light of the World. We cannot bemoan the fate of Gavroche and the other poor without the accompanying recognition that what we see is endemic, a betrayal of considerable magnitude, and that we are complicit in it. As Ecclestone points out succinctly, contrition cannot exist for the street urchin unless we see him as ours. It is "the old problem of coming naked to God, and for that to be truly a Yes of both joy and pain we need the new innocence of perception" (p. 50). Emphasized once more is the need to see, to perceive, to behold. For Hugo the great controversy, the war that is always being waged, is between Light and Darkness, between a society in which men and women die and rot in spiritual death because they walk in the dark rather than in the way of the one who is not only the Light of the World, but who has promised that those who follow him "will never walk in darkness but will have the light of life" (John 8:12).

The music of Gavroche and the wretched alerts the reader to things to be noticed, to the "beggars at [our] feet" who are indeed our fellows. This is not merely a call to notice something akin to us, but the assertion of an absolute identity. It is our "fellow man" who "lives on crumbs of humble piety" in the "slums of Saint Michel," in the slums everywhere. What is true when Jean Valjean sings that he will raise Cosette to the Light is true here as well. It is the power of that light which is Christ which will finally cut through the slums and reveal what has not been discerned. The darkness of ignorance which lives within the novel and on the stage can be probed and penetrated only by the light of God. What appears to be light and frivolous is considerably different from the reality. On the stage we are not aware that Gavroche and his brothers live inside the Bastille elephant and risk being eaten alive by rats, a paradigm of a reality which continues to exist, but Hugo offers us a clear vision of who we are and what our destiny will be if we fail to repudiate the darkness of sin and evil and embrace instead that Light which binds us to the reality of God.

That Gavroche is Eponine's brother and the Thenardier's son never surfaces in the musical, but the brief description of what passes for a family is offered by Hugo to suggest the state of darkness and sin in which the urchin lives.

> This was the family of our lively barefoot urchin. He went there to be greeted by poverty and wretchedness, and, which was worse, never a smile, by hearts as chilly as

the room itself. When he entered they asked where he had come from and he answered, 'off the streets'; when he left they asked where he was going and his answer was, 'back to the streets.' His mother asked, 'Why did you come here?'

The boy had grown up in this absence of affection like the pallid weeds that grow in cellars. His situation caused him no particular distress and he blamed no one. The fact is that he had no idea how parents ought to behave. (pp. 510-511)

In *The Complete Book of "Les Miserables,"* Edward Behr chronicles the history of the musical and acknowledges the debt owed to James Fenton, the original lyricist, who "wrote what concerned him" (p. 90) and whose works as a reporter in South-East Asia helped him to grasp that the street urchin of nineteenth century Paris shared a good deal with the "have-nots of Vietnam, the Philippines, Cambodia" (p. 90). Side by side the dark child of abuse and the world of the have-nots lies a warning from Hugo: "He watches prepared to laugh, but prepared also for other things. You who are Prejudice, Abuse, Ignominy, Oppression, Iniquity, Despotism, Injustice, Fanatacism, beware of the wide-eyed urchin. He will grow up" (p. 498).

Unfortunately, this warning in the form of a Gavroche lyric written by Fenton was lost when Kretzmer assumed the role of lyricist.

> You thought you would notice we had nothing to eat.
> You thought we wouldn't mind we had to sleep on the streets.
> You thought you wouldn't bother if we drank from a ditch.
> You thought we wouldn't wonder what had made you so rich.
> You made up all the rules.
> You must have thought us fools...
> You kicked us in the gutter and you laughed in our face.
> You dragged us through the courtroom and you taught us our place.
> You preached at us on Sunday looking solemn and sleek.
> You cheated us on Monday and the rest of the week.
> We saw the coaches passing on the way to the ball.
> I wonder if you noticed we had nothing at all.

We smelt you coming out again with brandy for breath.
I wonder if you noticed we were starving to death.
Be careful as you go.
You don't know what we know
You drove us to despair.
You thought we didn't care.

Here is an indictment embraced easily by Enjolras and the ABC in its revolutionary fervor, an acid criticism which ends with a warning, "be careful as you go," similar to Hugo's. If we think that those who abide with Gavroche in the high society of the slums won't "notice," "mind," "bother," or "wonder," we live under a delusion. The "gangsta rap" of today finds an antecedent in another lyric of Fenton's which was cut.

Ten little bullets in my hand,
ten little snipers neat and clean—
one for the king of this great land,
two for the aristocracee,
three for the bishops and the clergymen,
four for the prefects of police—

give me a chance, I'll take the lot of them—
ten little chances to be free.
Close your eyes, I'll say when, count to ten.

As Behr notes, the end result, unfortunately, is a more sentimental Gavroche rather than the street urchin who calls the reader to account for the life of the wretched.

On the stage, Gavroche becomes the one who welcomes the audience into Paris with him and subsequently announces the death of Lamarque, who uncovers the infiltration of Javert, and dies at the barricades all the while proclaiming what "little people can do." Even in its original version, Gavroche's song, "Little People," is a sanitized version of "You."

They laugh at me those fellas just because I am small
They laugh at me because I'm not a hundred feet tall
I tell them there's a lot to learn down here on the ground
The world is big but little people turn it around

A world can roll a stone, a bee can sting a bear,
A fly can fly around a sky cause flies don't care
A sparrow in a hut can make a happy home
A flea can bite the bottom of the pope in Rome
Goliath was a bruiser who was tall as the sky
But David threw a rock and gave him one in the eye
I never read the Bible but I know that it's true
It only goes to show what little people can do
So listen here professor with your head in the clouds
It's also kind of useful to get lost in a crowd
So people at universities don't give a damn
For better or for worse it's the way that I am
Be careful as you go cause little people grow
And little people know when little people fight
We might look easy pickings but we've got some bite
So never keep a dog because he's just a pup
You better run for cover when the pup grows up
And we'll fight like twenty armies and we won't give up.

Rather than a litany of charges against those who have created the beggars and the wretched, there exists a much more docile "be careful as you go cause little people grow" accentuated by the underdog David who slew Goliath and even this has been cut from the current productions so that all that remains is the final warning, "so you'd better run for cover when the pup grows up." Hugo asks us to take seriously Gavroche and Eponine, the street urchin and the wretched, to clear our minds in order to grasp what he tries to accomplish because such words as his and those in the musical become so much more than mere statements of information. Novelist and lyricist make statements which help to illuminate faith and proclaim that the world in which we live is in dire need of all the help which such artists can give.

In "Fern-Seed and Elephants," C. S. Lewis makes the point that there "are characters whom we know to be historical but of whom we feel that we do not have any personal knowledge—knowledge by acquaintance." For the purpose of *Les Miserables*, Lewis would probably include such figures as Napoleon and Ney and Lamarque. However, he continues, there are "others who make no claim to historical reality but whom, none the less, we know as we know real people": Valjean, Javert, Gavroche, and Eponine. I include the last two because, though not as fully developed as the hero and his adversary, they compel a response as well as the recognition that even under the harshest of conditions, within the family or without, and for reasons difficult to discern it is possible to retain a trace of love and to offer one's life for another.

This love manifests itself most openly in the figure of Eponine, a relatively minor figure in the novel, known for her subordinate role in the devilish planning of her father's criminal associates and her decision at the barricades to literally take a bullet that is meant for Marius. However, taking a liberty with what happens in the novel with regard to the letter which Marius sends to Cosette, she commands a much more significant role in the musical, especially in the poignantly despairing "On My Own" which captures her essential loneliness, not only as a young girl whose fortunes have plummeted since she first knew Cosette at her father's inn, but also as a woman whose love will never be repaid by the one she adores.

Our first introduction to Eponine occurs just before Fantine decides to ask the Thenardiers to care for Cosette. Only "about two and a half," Eponine and her sister Azelma appear well cared-for and give the appearance of "roses on a scrap-heap, their eyes bright, their pink cheeks round with laughter" as they are swung back and forth by their mother, "a woman of no very attractive appearance but likeable at that moment" (p. 145). At this moment, no hint is given of the pit into which Eponine will sink as the watchdog of the Patron-Minette. As a child she will be measured against Cosette and Cosette will always be found wanting until that later meeting when Eponine will recognize Cosette and exclaim "Cosette! Now I remember. Cosette! How can it be we were children together. Look what's become of me."

What has become of her is described carefully by Hugo when she delivers to Marius her father's letter requesting funds. In "Rose of the underworld," she retains some sense of the beauty that once appeared a birthright, a reminder that even beneath the most disfigured person some light can shine.

> She was a lean and delicate-looking creature, her shivering
> nakedness clad in nothing but a chemise and skirt. Her
> waistband was a piece of string, and another piece tied back
> her hair. Bony shoulders emerged from the chemise, and the
> face above them was sallow and flabby. The light fell upon
> reddened hands, a stringy neck, a loose depraved mouth
> lacking several teeth, bleared eyes both cold and wary: in
> short, an ill-treated girl with the eyes of a grown woman;
> a blend of fifty and fifteen; one of those creatures, at once
> weak and repellent, who cause those who set eyes on them
> to shudder when they do not weep. (p. 633)

In Eponine's world, spiritual values have no meaning almost to the
point that any concept of principle has become meaningless. There
appears to be no possibility for an occasion of God's presence, no
opportunity for revelation or epiphany, no chance for the eternal
fact of the Incarnation to be perceived in any sort of relationship.
Night would seem to have descended upon Eponine, a darkness
for which she is ill prepared, a darkness that is bound by the evil
that is her father and his cohorts.

Yet grace cannot so easily be eclipsed and the glory, which
lies dormant, manages to express itself imperfectly in her love for
Marius. While her father despises everything that is not himself,
she embraces human passion, sexuality, and warmth and, in her
own way, she repudiates the world embraced by Thenardier even
though, until her death, she cannot be totally free of it. When she
meets Marius later on, after she has procured Cosette's address,
she is still an unhappy girl, but her love for him has brought about
a transformation nearly as remarkable as Cosette's.

> Strangely, she appeared at once more impoverished and
> more attractive, two things which he would not have
> thought her capable of. She had progressed in two directions,
> both upwards and downwards. She was still barefoot and
> ragged as she had been on the day when she had marched
> so resolutely into his room, except that her rags were two
> months older, dirtier. Their tatters more evident. She had

the same hoarse voice, the same chapped, weather-beaten skin, the same bold and shiftless gaze, and added to these the apprehensive, vaguely pitiable expression that a spell in prison lends to the face of ordinary poverty. She had wisps of straw in her hair. Not because, like Ophelia, she had gone mad, but because she had spent the night in a stable-loft. And with it all she had grown beautiful! Such is the miracle of youth. (p. 752)

Such also is the miracle of love.

However, that miracle does not always erase the loneliness that invades a life, though in the end it will transform it. The most powerful expression of that loneliness in Eponine's life is reflected in the soliloquy "On My Own," a piece which echoes her description of her life to Marius in the novel. At times, she confesses, she goes out at night and doesn't come home. She even contemplates drowning herself, but thinks it would be too cold.

"I go off on my own when I feel like it and sleep in a ditch, likely as not. You know, at night when I'm walking along the boulevards the trees look to me like pitchforks, and the houses, they're so tall and black, like the towers of Notre-Dame, and when you come to a strip of white wall it's like a patch of water. And the stars are like street lamps and you'd think they were smoking, and sometimes the wind blows them out and I'm always surprised, as though a horse had come and snorted in my ear; and although it's night-time I think I can hear street-organs and the rattle of looms, and all kinds of things. And sometimes I think people are throwing stones at me and I run away and everything goes spinning round me. When you've had nothing to eat it's very queer. (Pp. 637-638)

The heart's ache accompanies the heart which throbs and we feel the pain, a grief which is part of her existence, woven into her life, and yet will be part of what Charles Williams calls the "web of glory" because her life will be sacrificial.

One of the remarkable things about the way in which "On My Own" is sung is that it is entirely consonant with Eponine's voice in the novel. When she attempts to make herself known to Marius in the novel, she strives "to make her voice soft but [can] only make it sound more guttural" so that "some of the words [get] lost in the passage from her throat to her lips, as on a piano with some of the notes missing" (p. 636) and later (in the passage cited above) she retains "the same hoarse voice" (p. 752).

After her death, Hugo recounts briefly the motivation and circumstances that led to it, noting especially the "sudden impulse" that had mastered her. It is an impulse born of her need-love which cries out from the poverty and loneliness of her life, an impulse to go to the barricade and "to plunge into that death" (p. 967). It is an impulse whose origin lies in her confession to Marius that sometimes she goes out at night and doesn't return home and whose agony springs from the impoverished and solitary life she is forced to live. When she stands alone on the stage, shrouded in mist, wrapped in her ancient rain coat, clutching herself, surrounded by wisps of light breaking through boarded up windows, her throaty voice cries out "and now I'm all alone again, nowhere to turn, no one to go to, without a home, without a friend, without a face to say hello to." The repetition of "without" accentuates the empty life in which she is trapped, a hell of its own characterized by suffering and cut adrift from any vision of glory. When she sings, it is as if she had lost her dignity and yet the paradox remains true—that in losing it she gains it, an empathy from reader and audience who discover that such fragmentation and solitude, such desolation and devastation compel the need to shape anew forms of life which resist all that leads to despair.

In her dream of Marius, which has echoes of Fantine's "I Dreamed a Dream," Eponine changes her surroundings and invests them with wonder only to have them become bare and empty when the night is over and she can live no longer in her imagination. We need to note the recurrent images of the dream: "make believe," "live inside my head," "pretending he's beside me," "only in my mind," "I've only been pretending," and "on my own." They bear witness to the emptiness of a life without love which can find hope solely in the imagination. "On My Own" has become a Broadway standard, a familiar text that threatens to dull the truth that it expresses by virtue of its very familiarity. Eponine's longing for Marius is ultimately a longing for God and though she would never work this out theologically it is true, even in the impure sacrifice that she makes as she hopes that if she can't have Marius neither will anyone else, that through this narrow slit in space and time the love of God is poured out into the world through one girl's suffering.

Even when it is tinged with selfishness and possessiveness, any act of selflessness proceeds from the very heart of God so that while it is erroneous as far as the novel is concerned, it is entirely appropriate to the musical that the dead Eponine appear with Fantine beside Valjean in the finale. From all eternity, such salvation is seen and Eponine's reception of the bullet meant for Marius is a small re-enactment of Christ's sacrifice writ large in the sky above the barricade. In her death, intimacy is achieved finally not only with Marius but also with God. What was once empty and desolate is now given identity and meaning and she becomes part of that co-inherent life which extends beyond the barricades.

In the novel, a nobility exists in Eponine's death, a nobility that comes across in her final words: "You know, Monsieur Marius, I think I was a little bit in love with you" (p. 966). These words conclude her dialogue with Marius at the barricade, a conversation punctuated by her delivery of the letter. Hers is a martyrdom born of love, in the name of love, and transfigured by love. The offering of herself for another secures her redemption and her death is a triumph. Her love has moved from an infatuation expressed in a croaking voice while Marius lay hidden under a bed in the Gorbeau tenement to a substantial awareness that true love does "forever last, for ever, ever, ever last!" (p. 669).

Gavroche and Eponine draw us into an intimate communion with the rejected and in so doing remind us that there must be nothing static about such a communion. For them, in the midst of their poverty, desolation, and loneliness, life is still a journey, a process that will lead "through death into life, life in this world and life in the world beyond this one, 'an eternal progress into the inexhaustible riches of the divine life'" (*Participation in God*, p. 6).

Chapter 12

An Uprising Against Disorder:
Love as Prayer

Early in *Les Miserables*, Jean Valjean wrestles with his conscience as he seeks to resolve the dilemma of the tempest which resides within him: whether to reveal who he is and save Champmathieu or keep his identity a secret. Once that conundrum has been solved, once he has become free from the shackles of prison for a second time, once he discovers the power of love in the person of Cosette, he believes in some measure that his life is complete, that nothing can intrude on the joy and peace he has found in Fantine's daughter. Interruptions occur, some miraculous and melodramatic escapes are necessary, but love is secure since Cosette is "his." The horror lies in the possessive, the failure to realize as yet that people are not meant to be possessed, that love exists truly only where freedom and obedience lie side by side in mutual exchange. When Valjean discovers Marius' existence and recalls the signals that he has missed, his emotions are violent, and when he reads surreptitiously Marius' letter to Cosette, he is conscious only of the following: "I shall die....When you read this my soul will be very near" (p. 980).

At this moment Hugo tells us that before Jean Valjean's eyes lies a marvel: "the death of the hated person" (p. 980). However, when a man such as Valjean has had his life touched by selfless love, the subsequent transformation is accompanied by the discovery that such love is not merely an essential component of existence but its very root and must be expressed without compromise in one's daily life. For a man who has come slowly and with great pain to view his journey as a movement toward the redemptive love and power of the Cross, selflessness must replace selfishness. Hence, his initial response to the crucial lines in Marius' letter does not bring him the tranquility and peace that he assumes will be his.

> ...Valjean felt that he was saved. Once again he would have Cosette to himself, without any rival, and then life together would continue as before. He had only to keep this letter in his pocket. Cosette would never know what had happened to that other man. "I have only to let things take their course. There is no escape for the youth. If he is not yet dead he will certainly die. What happiness!"
>
> But having assured himself of this, Valjean's gloom returned; and presently he went downstairs and roused the porter. (p. 981)

That gloom is the consequence of a conscience awake and born of the inner realization that such happiness is merely a delusion. Thus he decides to don his uniform and make his way to the barricade, a decision that can arise only out of a life that has begun to be lived as a prayer. Love, compassion, conscience, and commitment conquer false happiness and Valjean is once again set free by God's grace while Javert, now a spy, remains imprisoned by the letter of the law. Having undergone his own exodus from a world which, he believes initially, seeks revenge, Valjean must now reject what appears to be a moment of victory and venture instead into the unknown. He does not know what will transpire, but he does know that in the midst of this desert which he has chosen to enter he will not be alone, that desolation and despair are not possibilities for those who know God no matter what one's whimsical, capricious, and untrustworthy emotions may proclaim at any given moment.

Valjean's choice to venture to the barricade arises from his strong conviction that the focus of one's gaze must be fixed on the one for whom the bishop has purchased his soul, on the one who has delivered him from sin, from a life bent on hatred and the execution of vengeance. The vulnerability of God, dramatized on the Cross, brings with it the accompanying awareness that the "way home is by learning to be of service to others" (*Passion for Pilgrimage*, p. 94), that vulnerability is a condition of the converted life on the road to Calvary. Steeped more and more in this conviction, he will be able not only to set Javert free, but also to pray for Marius' life, even at the expense of his own, and subsequently carry the severely wounded young man through the sewers of Paris. The choice which Valjean makes now to free one enemy and to offer himself for one whom he believes to be another enhances those earlier decisions which suggest the interconnectedness of all people—the rescue of Fauchelevant, his old foe, from under the runaway cart and the saving of Champmathieu at Arles—and accentuates the fact that "God on the Cross places us in each other's care" (*Passion for Pilgrimage*, p. 94). This is expressed on the stage in the hauntingly beautiful musical prayer, "Bring Him Home."

Suffused in a beam of light, Valjean sits on an ammunition box and expresses through the falsetto tones of the song a strong sense that he resides within God's all-embracing love, that the Passion and the Blood identified by the bishop in the Prologue are now a constant in his life. As Valjean raises his voice to "God on high," he does so with the certainty that God has "always been there." He owns for himself a faith of which so many can only talk because his engagement with God has been personal, an exchange which has become an "ever-deepening communion" with someone whom he believes is always ready to be with him as He hears his call. In a sense, he articulates in the simple lyrics of his soliloquy what is an underlying religious principle found throughout the text: that, in Karl Barth's words, "to clasp the hands in prayer is the beginning of an uprising against the disorder of the world," that when with Gregory the Great, "the soul strengthens itself by prayer, it is united to the one who listens on high." As he lifts his hands, his heart, and his voice, Valjean utters his Yes to all that he has encountered thus far in his life.

> In the triumph of prayer
> Twofold is the spell.

With the folding of hands
There's a spreading of wings
And the soul's lifted up to invisible lands
And ineffable peace. Yet it knows, being there
That it's close to the heart of all pitiful things;
And it loses and finds, and it gives and demands;
For its life is divine, it must love, it must share
In the triumph of prayer.
                    (quoted in *Lent with Evelyn Underhill*, p. 13)

As the Bishop of Digne affirmed his trust in Christ, so Valjean sings his faith in the presence and power of God to meet any need, to equip the petitioner for the exigencies of the moment. Having learned, almost intuitively and certainly imaginatively from the example of the holy bishop, Valjean's belief, vague and undefined early in his journey, has now been deepened. The intense emotion that attends this moment is not an accurate barometer for this newfound depth, but the immediate recognition of God's immanence suggests that God has let the bucket down into the depths of Jean Valjean (to borrow C. S. Lewis' metaphor in *Letters to Malcolm, Chiefly on Prayer*).

Part of the power of *Bring Him Home* lies in its expression of dependence on God not as some sort of supernatural defense against imminent danger, but as an omnipotent power whose love will enable him to face the danger. We learn in the novel and the musical of the struggles that exist within Jean Valjean, of the demons who wrestle with the angels for possession of his soul, and one of the glories of Valjean's prayer is that it conveys the essence of this internal battle. The man who would desire Marius dead now prays that he be brought home, that if death is to take place that it be his own rather than Marius' – "Greater love hath no man...." As he relinquishes his hatred of Marius, Valjean's prayer expresses a truth which perceived from within can be expressed only in music. In love, says Karl Rahner, the gates of the soul spring open, as they do for Valjean, and the singing of this prayer articulates that new freedom and wholeness which enable him to forget the pettiness of his jealousy. Valjean's entire being pours forth like a living stream that has irrigated the rigid desert of what he once was and releases him from the prison he has constructed for himself by virtue of his animosity toward Marius.

The power of the language in this song and of the journey which is at the heart of the novel resides neither in the resonant quality of the caressed strings of a harp nor in the strength of the singer's voice. These provide only a visceral response, a reaction which is perhaps momentary and superficial, and certainly emotional. The real power lies in the simplicity of the words and the conviction which conveys them because, as Alan Ecclestone suggests in *Yes to God* (p. 19), those words possess heart and mind and mouth, because they profess a pervasive love which exists in the dynamic "give-and-take between the little [soul] of [Jean Valjean] and that three-fold Reality" (*Lent with Evelyn Underhill*, p. 23) which is the Trinity.

What we discover here is that the individual, the one who tries desperately, in the midst of temptation and weakness, to live his life as a prayer, whose life becomes his prayer, is at work at all moments uttering his affirmation of God's presence in his life. His prayer is not at all unlike what the ancient Celts called the "Caim" or the "Encircling." David Adam notes that when the Celtic saints were confronted with evil they would draw a circle, or "Caim," around them to express the reality of the Presence of God. To do this is to move, as Valjean does, to that point in one's existence where reality can be wrestled with in such a way that life is enhanced in the midst of whatever threatens that life. Marius might indeed have been wished dead in the despair of the moment, but now, with utmost sincerity and trust, Valjean can desire for him peace and joy. H. A. Williams makes the point in *The Joy of God* that such a desire can arise only from the recognition that God dwells within one and thus, our wills, cooperating as with Jean Valjean's, creates "our true selves and establishes our personal identity" (p. 20) Thus, rather than an antagonist, he becomes like a son and one would not wish for a son an adder. In his prayer, Valjean summons from the recesses of his turbulent self all that is with regard to Marius and brings it before that God who is nearer to Valjean than the air he breathes, whose presence "is not something he has earned but is a free gift" (*The Joy of God*, p. 20). During the stage production, one must summon memory in order to recall that in the midst of this petition to "bring him home" there is both light and dark, joy and pain, life and death. To clasp his hands on behalf of Marius is to venture beyond the immediacy of the moment and to engage himself with the creative and reconciling love of God in Christ. To choose to act in such a manner is to become deeply aware that eternity penetrates time, that God on high is also God at hand, that God transcendent is also God immanent, the one who in the humility of the Incarnation enters into humanity and transforms it.

Pain and love reside side by side in one's life, the pain of that vulnerability which can be found only in the gift of one's heart to another. However, that pain and love exist also side by side on the Cross and when one recognizes the congruence then the prayer uttered at the barricade of any life seeks entrance into and resolution of that which lies in the depths of the often chaotic but always yearning self. To cite Ecclestone once more, prayer of this sort holds the pray-er (and his concerns of whatever kind) as much as it can in the light of God and his truth (p. 7).

Here Hugo is like an architect breaking new ground because Valjean seeks desperately a world made new, one that is transfigured so that his hands are "made new to handle holy things, his wrists as fresh and pure as water from a well," to borrow a phrase from Muir's *The Transfiguration*. In this desire, he begins to discover a voice within, the Holy Spirit uttering "Abba, Father," a voice that is authentic because it is obedient to the promptings of the Spirit and the heart. In the selfless request to "Bring [Marius] home," we discern not just what may appear to be a resolution to a difficult and dangerous predicament, a situation that is so precarious that it hangs, quite literally, by the thread of a prayer, but an implied willingness to live out whatever transpires. As he lifts his eyes to heaven, Valjean focuses his attention on God, on him who is the light of the world, the way, the truth, and the life. For Jean Valjean, God is near at hand, never remote, and his words convey the substantial fact that his role at the barricade will be carried out under the aegis of God and in his power.

Valjean's prayer is petition, but it is also an act of recognition that God alone takes and gives. His "if I die, let me die" acts as a kind of surrender of the self accompanied by the fervent plea that Marius live. As Ecclestone remarks about this sort of prayer, it is an inner desire on the part of the one who prays to "see things in that true light which is [God's] glory" (*Yes to God*, p. 9), or as C. S. Lewis expresses it in a letter, it is quite useless to knock at the door of heaven for mere comfort in the present situation, because such earthly comfort is not what is supplied there (*The Letters of C. S. Lewis*, p. 290). As the bishop chooses freely to anchor firmly his entire existence in the fact of God in Christ, no matter the moral, political, and economic climate in which he must live, so Jean Valjean is now able to face the terrible dilemma of Marius with at first openness, then compassion, and finally love. That is why he is able now to say "in my need/You have always been there." This is an explicit echo of Jesus' prayer in Gethsemane, a model for all prayer, and his high priestly prayer in John 17 and, for Valjean, a staggering assertion that our knowledge and apprehension of Christ's love for us is the ground of our existence. As the Cross is the glory of God, so is Valjean's willingness to sacrifice himself for Marius the highest expression of that love and, as William Temple notes in his commentary on John's Gospel, the glory which attends any man's offer of himself on behalf of another is complete in the offer even if no consequence attends it. Valjean's prayer here is that intercommunication between himself and God, an exchange that will be heightened and deepened in the musical's Finale and the final pages of the novel.

Because Jean Valjean's initial desire for revenge against the world that always hated him, a world that attempted to murder him by replacing his name with a number and thus robbing him of an identity, a world that "chained [him] and left [him] for dead," has been transformed by the grace of God and the compassion of the bishop to an intense desire to love, he is now able to assimilate into his life that gospel by which one must live if sense is to be made ultimately of existence. Thus "God on high, hear my prayer" is a cry for help, a desperate call which could not have been made before the encounter with the bishop because God, the wholly Other, would never have been acknowledged in faith and hope. Like the Psalmist, Valjean can now cry out in pain and joy because he knows that God knows and loves him in all his complexity.

> O Lord, you have searched me and known me.
> You know when I sit down and when I rise up;
> you discern my thoughts from far away.
> You search out my path and my lying down,
> and are acquainted with all my ways.
> Even before a word is on my tongue,
> O Lord, you know it completely.
> You hem me in, behind and before,
> and lay your hand upon me.
> Such knowledge is too wonderful for me;
> it is so high that I cannot attain it.
>
> (Psalm 139:1-5, NRSV)

The psalm and the song are a prayer that expresses truth and the song attempts to enter the depths that reside deep within him with regard to Marius. He is willing to be called out of those depths in order to be molded into a new creation in Christ, a step he has taken previously and will take again. It is as if he were saying something akin to "I give thanks to you, O God, that I have risen this day. I surrender myself to you and as I do so I rise to life itself. May the day that dawns be a blessing. Help me to avoid any act which may separate me from you." Whatever happens at the barricade—life or death, freedom or imprisonment, for himself and/or for Marius—Valjean can now attend to and respond to that conversation which will help him to participate actively in whatever existence offers because he knows that God has traveled already every highway which is Valjean's journey.

> Where can I go from your spirit?
> Or where can I flee from your presence?
> If I ascend to heaven, you are there;
> if I make my bed in Sheol, you are there.

If I take the wings of the morning and
settle at the farthest limits of the sea,
even there your hand shall lead me,
And your right hand shall hold me fast. (Psalm 139:6-9)

As Adam points out in *Border Lands*, the one who journeys in Christ does not know what lies ahead or where he will go or what the future holds, but he does know *Who* is with him and *Who* is there before him (p. 100 – see also Alan Ecclestone, *Yes to God*, for a further exploration of this principle).

As one sits in the comfort of a theater seat, perhaps securely distanced from what transpires on the stage, one is nevertheless still struck with the chord of longing which resonates from "Bring Him Home." Somehow, if we will surrender to what is at hand, open our hearts and minds to it, we can manage to become one with Jean Valjean as our perhaps often desperate selves unite with him and we recognize that his prayer and ours are said and sung in the blessed assurance that God has all eternity in which to enter into them, that we and our concerns are very real to him. Valjean does not attempt to "dress himself in borrowed robes," to use language that is not his, but says simply "here I am Lord, at your mercy, committed to your care." His act of engagement with God is intensely personal, wrung out of himself with agonizing cost. If attended to closely it can be heard and felt in Hugo's prose as well as in the musical, and because the engagement is so genuine the new Valjean who emerges is completely convincing. As at every crucial moment in his life, as with all of us, he is the clay in the hands of the potter being shaped and molded to perfection, journeying with the saints in the ever more clear recognition that "our hearts will find no rest until they rest in Thee."

Throughout *Les Miserables*, Hugo affirms that God, author and creator, the one who has designed his creation to be in harmony with him, is with us from the beginning of time though we, fallen as we are, choose a note other than the one which he has authored. When such discord occurs, his companionship may be hidden and often secret until some act or engagement unlocks what we have heretofore chosen to keep imprisoned. When Valjean chooses to go to the barricade, when he utters his prayer, he chooses to set aside the personal and surrender himself to God. Because he has chosen to try to obey and adore, grace and love dissolve bitterness and possessiveness. Valjean is receptive to an internal knowledge, one learned through love and engagement with God and tried in the fires of inner struggle rather than acquired merely through the intellect. Consequently, in his desire to attempt to rescue Marius, he is willing to risk a venture into the "cloud of unknowing," into the darkness of trust (*True Prayer*, p. 22). As Kenneth Leech points out so accurately about prayer, with trust as the mainspring of his outpouring to God on Marius' behalf, it is not so much that his intercession is some sort of attempt to alter the mind of God, but is instead a "releasing of God's power through placing [himself] in a relationship of cooperation with God" (p. 25).

If Valjean had ever become complacent, if he had ever made the decision to forsake the life he had chosen to live in the "Presence of God," whether in Montreuil-sur-mer, the Petit-Picpus, or the Rue Plumet, he could have become dead to prayer. However, he has learned, almost intuitively from the bishop's response to him (and we from the bishop's engagement with the poor and disenfranchised), that prayer is entwined inextricably with struggle, that to be deaf to such needs as those expressed by the "miserables" is to be dead to prayer. Consequently, as he gives to the poor and puts himself at Fantine's disposal, as he adopts and loves Cosette and offers himself on behalf of Marius, Valjean illustrates Thomas Merton's belief that such engagement permits "prayer to pray within you, whether you know it or not."

As Valjean completes his prayer and dawn breaks at the barricade, one is struck by a sense of serenity in the midst of uncertainty. God is always there, in Christ, in the suffering, because the Cross, the ultimate means of agony and suffering, remains the way to oneness with God. In that Cross which towers over all creation and which is at the heart of all life and all prayer, one is free to intercede for others and offer oneself on their behalf.

For Fantine and Cosette and Marius, Valjean stands between them and God and as he was raised to the light by the bishop, he does the same for them and in so doing he becomes "a house for the divine presence." Such is the effect of prayer; such is the beginning of that uprising against the world's chaos. In "Bring Him Home," we participate in the altering of one man's perspective, a moment, which conveys all that has been recalled of the past and a moment in which the future is surrendered to God. Perhaps A. M. Allchin expresses the position best at the beginning of *The Living Presence of the Past.*

> The practice of prayer proves to be not only or even primarily a matter of giving comfort to the emotions or providing stimulus to the will, but of bringing light and understanding to the mind, providing serious illumination of man's relationship with God, and of his situation in this world in which he finds himself. (p. 3)

At this juncture in the novel and at this moment on the stage, Jean Valjean holds together the timeless and constant love of God which hearkens to each prayer and his own immediate concern with Marius and his life is transcended. Not only that, Hugo and Kretzmer invite us to become contemporaneous with Valjean. As H. A. Williams notes, we do not say about Valjean "there but for the grace of God go I," but "there I am."

"Bring Him Home" marks a penultimate moment on Jean Valjean's journey toward Calvary and that journey will be completed in the final pages of the novel and the final scene of the musical as the song is reprised though with several changes in the language. As he dies, his prayer has brought him to that point where he is ready now to enter what Ecclestone calls the "as yet unspoken, unseen, unimaginable Yes whither Christ has gone before" (*Yes to God*, p. 4). Indeed, God brings him home.

Chapter 13

Javert's Suicide:
To Choose the Abyss

In the musical, just before he sings his prayer for Marius, Jean Valjean encounters Javert, now taken prisoner by the ABC. In the novel, it is a confrontation which has an ominous hint to it because Valjean's figure casts such a shadow that Javert must turn his head and only manage simply, "So here we are" (p. 1008) as he averts coolly the gaze of his long sought quarry. A subtle change is evident in the aversion, but not yet one that is sufficient to erase that equanimity, even arrogance, which is such an integral part of Javert's character and which he is able to maintain even in the face of anticipated death. Certain of his righteousness, he is rendered nearly speechless and is unable to conceal his amazement when Valjean cuts the ropes and sets him free.

We need to recollect what we know of Javert in order to grasp the essence of this amazement. Born in a jail, choosing to embrace the law as an absolute, Hugo makes us aware that his wilderness exists within, that he has embraced an arid existence which has no promise of any oasis for rest, peace, or spiritual refreshment. Always secretive, forever on a case, he is the consummate hunter always on the prowl for his prey. In the form of the criminal, that prey is utterly predictable, its actions beyond surprise. His rigid assessment of any felon, and specifically Jean Valjean, is consistent with his perception of an ordered world: "Once a thief, forever a thief. What you want you always steal!"

However, such perception, in spite of an apparent moral rectitude and attendant belief in a God of justice, indicates the depth of Javert's sin. When Valjean requests of Enjolras control over Javert's life--"Give me the spy Javert—Let me take care of him!" and "That I may be allowed to blow that man's brains out" (p. 1038)--every tenet of Javert's carefully orchestrated world seems confirmed. Then, suddenly, like a bolt of lightning from a clear sky, the hunted not only relinquishes its pursuer but frees him. Valjean sees clearly where Javert does not and in the release he witnesses to the clarity of his vision, a witness that has the Incarnation as its heart and God's immensity, intimacy, and transcendent glory as its root. As Allchin notes in *Living Presence of the Past*, "all that causes men and women to hate and seek to destroy is overcome by God's life-giving power of reconciliation and peace expressed in Christ" (p. 121) if they will only have it so. Though no evidence exists in the text that Hugo knows explicitly of the doctrine of exchange and substitution as a theological truth, such a doctrine is evident in the acts of Jean Valjean.

Having become aware personally of that gracious God who is "the comfort of all who sorrow, the strength of all who suffer," Valjean hears the cry of those in misery and in need and, in the words of *The Book of Common Prayer*, is given "the strength to serve them for the sake of him who suffered for us" (*The Book of Common Prayer*, p. 279). Such insight is the consequence of the confession of one's blindness and the resulting opening of one's eyes to behold and accept the light and walk by it. Valjean continues to affirm his integrity as he releases Javert, an act that arises out of his commitment to journey toward God, to journey into Christ and his Cross. In the release, he offers Javert a creative and life-affirming act as an experience which, if he will abandon his cynicism and embrace it in love and with reconciliation, will begin to resurrect him from his dead past and present. Such is the freedom of Valjean's offer that it is made without "conditions, bargains, or petitions."

In the full recognition that he is "a man no worse than any man," as well as a man who has reversed the process of his sin,

Jean Valjean understands that "forgiveness is the public virtue of Christianity, the exact opposite of vengeance, a process of action and reaction, [which] brings about a new chain of relationship by introducing a new and unpredictable factor into the situation" (*True Prayer*, p. 130). Having been literally brought to his knees in tears and having gathered to himself the reconciling acts of God mediated through the bishop, Valjean is able, as Grossman notes, to treat others, strangers and adversaries, the wretched and Javert, as if they were brothers and thus he continues to triumph over the "evil that lurks within" (p. 42). Valjean can sing without any qualms that Javert is "wrong and always [has] been wrong," but Javert, his conscience darkened, cannot comprehend the possibility that the God who forgives each man from the Cross now dwells within Valjean.

Javert's narrow perspective cannot conceive of such a re-born existence, will not admit that Valjean could possibly immerse himself in the love of God though the evidence is before his eyes. Javert chooses blindness and that blindness binds him to his sin and his sin to him. It is as if he has become immune to the reconciling love of God whereas Valjean looks now with his eyes open wide so that he begins to see the world and all that dwells therein as a manifestation of the Light. His re-birth is never viewed as a finished product and thus he can look upon Javert and behold what Javert himself cannot see: the light of God. When Valjean sings "clear out of here" and "there's nothing that I blame you for" and says "you're free to go," then adding where he can be found, he offers Javert an opportunity to transform his life and his personality, a transformation in the personal and the spiritual order. That the chapter which chronicles Javert's release should be titled "The vengeance of Jean Valjean" is a powerful use of irony. The felon who begins his life out of jail bent on revenge now actuates that vengeance through an act of mercy, compassion, and love, an act that the self-assured, self-satisfied, and self-possessed Javert cannot grasp. He finds the act "embarrassing", so deeply has it penetrated his inflexible intellectual certainty. He would rather that Valjean had killed him (p. 1040) than that his own convictions be exposed to doubt. It is as if he finds it impossible not only that such a man could love, but also that he is even lovable and the end result is that he turns initially on Valjean and then finally on himself.

While Valjean recognizes at first implicitly and then explicitly that he owes everything he has and has become to God, the one who gave "him hope when hope was gone" and "strength to journey on," Javert refuses to accept the agony and pain of intellectual doubt. As we shall see shortly, Javert's decision is a refusal to live because, as H. A. Williams notes, to live "means dying to the world as the intellectual possession of our closed-up ego in order to rediscover it by meeting and communicating with it" (*True Resurrection*, p. 95). Whereas Javert refuses such a death, Valjean undergoes another kind of baptism that is itself a death as he carries Marius through the sewers.

> "To go into the sewer is to go into the grave," men said. All sorts of legends covered that colossal sink with horror, that dreadful place which bears the impress of the revolution of the earth and of men, in which the remains of every cataclysm is to be found, from the Flood to the death of Marat. (p. 1075)

Shortly thereafter, Hugo tells us that Valjean "had moved from one circle of Hell into another" (p. 1077). It is as if he had become a Dante journeying through an eternal place where all history is present in its fallenness (Hugo notes that "history flows through the sewer"--p. 1065) and one can hear the lamentation of lost souls, but for Valjean the road through the sewers of Hell will not be a final resting place. Instead the judgment of death will also be the occasion for new life, not only for him but also for Marius. It is one more occasion for initiation into that new life which has been imaged as a "never-ending road to Calvary," one more occasion which proclaims that such an immersion is under God's protection no matter how deep "the cave of evil mists and pitfalls" (p. 1077), and one more occasion from which Valjean is able to rise anew because he bears the seal of the Holy Spirit in his heart. He is "Jonah in the body of the whale" (p. 1079), but also much more than Jonah. As he carries Marius, he is "hungry and thirsty, especially thirsty, in that place of water where there was none to drink" (p. 1084) and he reminds us of Christ on the Cross bearing the sins of the world. Indeed, Hugo titles the chapter of the journey through the cloaca "He too bears his cross" (V, iii, 4, p. 1084).

As Valjean moves across the stage, light barely entering through the grates above him, water dripping in the background, the darkness threatens to pierce his soul as he lives out the law of substitution: "bear ye one another's burdens and so fulfill the law of Christ" Galatians 6:2). Yet such a threat, intensified by his movement through the sludge which threatens to swallow him in its filth and thus humiliate him because "filth is synonymous with shame, squalid and infamous" (p. 1087), becomes miraculously an occasion for redemption as Valjean sees the way of escape. As the clear light of day enters the sewer and escape appears imminent, Valjean's feelings become those "of a damned soul seeing the way out of Hell" (p. 1089). Grossman comments that "by pursuing his unerring moral course, even to the foulest of depths, Jean Valjean emerges so utterly transfigured that no one recognizes him afterward" (p. 43). But safety is not yet his and though he escapes Thenardier, who fails to recognize him, Javert is there, "the faithful servant at his post once more."

In the ensuing exchange, Valjean, "the man of mercy," pleads successfully for Marius and then asks Javert for one last favor: "Let me go home for a minute. After that you can do what you like with me" (p. 1098). Such a surrender is a capitulation to God and to suffering as well as to a world dominated by law and justice rather than love and compassion, but in that willingness to embrace vulnerability and all the pain which accompanies it lies a fidelity which leads at the end to the glory of God's kingdom. What follows is not in the musical, but it is of the utmost importance because it emphasizes the disparity between the two antagonists. Hugo calls it the "Collapse of the absolute."

> Where he personally was concerned, all was over. He had been taken by Javert and had made no resistance. Another man in his place might have thought of the rope Thenardier had given him and the bars of the first prison cell he would enter; but since his first encounter with the bishop there was in Valjean a profound religious abhorrence of any act of violence, even against himself. Suicide, that mysterious plunge into the unknown, which might entail some degree of death of the soul, was impossible for Jean Valjean. (p. 1098)

Suicide is impossible for Jean Valjean because he has a source "beyond the inner citadel of the self" while the same is not true for Javert whose only source is the unyielding letter of the law.

Part V, Book Four is a single chapter with a title which implies the state of Javert's mind—"Javert in Disarray"—and mirrors precisely the inner turbulence which torments Valjean in "A tempest in a human skull." What follows is perhaps the key passage in the chapter.

> He could see two ways ahead of him, and this appalled him, because hitherto he had never seen more than one straight line. And the paths led in opposite directions. One ruled out the other. Which was the true one?
>
> To owe his life to a man wanted by the law and to pay the debt in equal terms; to have accepted the words, "you may go," and now to say, "Go free," this was to sacrifice duty to personal motive, while at the same time feeling that the personal motive had a wider and perhaps higher application; it was to betray society while keeping faith with his own conscience. That this dilemma should have come upon him was what so overwhelmed him. He was amazed that Valjean should have shown him mercy, and that he should have shown Valjean mercy in return.
>
> And now what was he to do? It would be bad to arrest Valjean, bad also to let him go. In the first case an officer of the law would be sinking to the level of the criminal, and in the second the criminal would be rising above the law. There are occasions when we find ourselves with an abyss on either side, and this was one of them. (Pp. 1104-1105)

When Valjean wrestles earlier in the novel, he triumphs over the inner voices which tempt him to safety first and which urge a merely logical solution to the problem of Champmathieu. The end is different for Javert who prefers the solitude of his own self-created Hell rather than face the possibility of a new beginning offered him by Valjean and so he leans forward from the parapet on which he stands and drops into the darkness: "There was a splash, and that was all" (p. 1109).

As omniscient author, Hugo conveys the turbulence of the debate which rages within Javert and that turbulence is captured powerfully on the stage. Hugo has Javert ponder whether there could be other things "in life besides trials and sentences, authority and the police" (p. 1105) while Kretzmer has him wonder whether Valjean can be believed. Javert has been offered a glimpse of his true identity, but rather than appropriate for himself the vision held up by Jean Valjean, he chooses to see only a devil rather than a messenger from God. He is offered an opportunity to make a surrender of faith, but his pride refuses it. No Kierkegaardian leap for him in the midst of doubt; no recognition that such trust is at the heart of a whole personality. Only a deafness to the call of God which is due to a deep defect within him.

Those moments exist in some lives when one comes face to face with truth, acknowledges that truth, and refuses it anyway. A chilling illustration of this occurs in C. S. Lewis' fairy tale for grown-ups, *That Hideous Strength*, when Frost "comes to know and simultaneously refuses the knowledge" and then burns himself to death. Javert's suicide is similar. His life and principles in disarray, his inner self in turmoil, Hugo describes him as entertaining some sort of undefined concept of love and mercy as he contemplates in amazement Valjean's generosity toward him: "Something dreadful was forging its way into Javert's consciousness" (p. 1106).

Throughout the novel, Javert has thought of himself as part of the harmony of the created order, certain of the law which has dictated his life, and this belief is expressed in the musical in "Stars." Now his certainty has been shattered and this, according to Hugo, is his greatest anguish. He who has "never doubted all those years" now begins to doubt, to acknowledge that he can feel, to see clearly that the "monstrosity" which was once the convicted felon is now deserving of "admiration," and an inner voice convicts him as he affirms that the law was the law and nothing could be "more simple than to enforce it" (p. 1106).

> But when he sought to raise his hand to lay it on Valjean's shoulder an inner voice restrained him: "You will deliver up your deliverer? Then go and find Pontius Pilate's bowl and wash your hands!" He felt himself diminished beside Jean Valjean. (p. 1106)

What is happening to Javert resembles the "de-railing of a train—the straight line of the soul broken by the presence of God. God, the inwardness of man, the true conscience as opposed to the false; the eternal, splendid presence" (p. 1107).

In his soliloquy which prefaces his suicide, Javert sings "Damned if I'll live in the debt of a thief. Damned if I'll yield at the end of the chase." Perfectly congruent with what transpires in the novel, it is obvious that Javert will not embrace what appears to him to be incomprehensible no matter the weight of the facts. The shifts in the music and Javert's untying of his hair capture Hugo's observation that "he felt that his head must explode" (p. 1107). His release by Jean Valjean has made his life a hell, one that he could change, but to do so requires a denial of all that he has embraced, and so he chooses to remain in Hell. It is as if the demonic strikes at him with such force that he is compelled to arrive at the conclusion that love and mercy, God-given facts though they may be, are an absurdity.

The stars which shone once with certainty, with order and light, are now "black and cold" and he must "stare into the void of a world that cannot hold" law and mercy, love and justice in creative tension. Unable to reconcile paradox, Javert must embrace suicide because "There is nowhere [he] can go. There is no way [for him] to go on." The irony is that the man who would be just is unjust to himself. He refuses the law of grace, which has been offered freely and which he has been set free to follow in the strength that

Christ supplies. Rather than be set free, he invokes damnation and damnation does not disappoint. Such sin, such evil, is a matter of invitation in the face of the evidence, a conscious decision to set one's heart and mind against the offer of hope and a new life. It results in a loss of hope and renders Javert in the end cold and lifeless, dead, producing nothing, himself a void. He is like Charles Williams's Lawrence Wentworth as he climbs steadfastly down a rope toward that emptiness which is Hell refusing firmly every offer of redemption during the course of the descent. In Williams's words, "he descended into the bottomless circles of the void." Misguided as he is, Javert loves the law more than the Lawgiver and thus, as he drops into the Seine, he moves from the last flickering bits of light into the world of night, perhaps even, in Dante's vision, into the world of eternal suicide.

Not unlike Dante's Pier delle Vigne, Javert would rather be dead than live in humiliation because all the principles that he embraced have been repudiated in the person of Jean Valjean, "now deserving of veneration" (p. 1106). The world Javert has known is now "lost in shadow" and the rigid absolute is now more a withered sterility. The mystery of God's redemptive love forever escapes Javert. This is not sufficient to condemn him. However, while such a mystery must remain somehow inexplicable, it is possible to behold the mystery, to live it, and to discover its truth. In the penitent and redeemed Jean Valjean, Javert comes face to face with an occasion for grace, even for praise. Such an occasion illustrates what Paul Tillich meant in *The Shaking of the Foundation* when he wrote that sometimes in moments of great pain and restlessness "a wave of light breaks into our darkness" and makes us aware that a voice is telling us that we are accepted by that which is greater than we are (cited in *Christian Meditations*, p. 115). Herein lies the opportunity for Javert to say Yes to God's grace, to refuse that self-hatred which has risen within him, to begin a new journey to the throne of grace. Yet even as he perceives this from within, his refusal to act on it, to have stirred within him a penitent longing for understanding and fuller faith is the final failure. The decision to say no to this perception, to reject the God who in Christ reconciles the fallen world to himself is to remain imprisoned in the false god of the law. What he will not grasp is that it is only by opening himself to accept that grace which is offered freely that he will be able to reject the rigidity of the law which has bound and imprisoned him. As we have discovered with Valjean time and again, the grace of God has the power to change the reality it encounters, but when that change fails to occur, as with Javert, grace has been rejected.

The Javert we meet in the novel and on the stage becomes at the end not someone to be feared, but to be pitied, prayed for, and ultimately loved because it is love which gives life. When he sings "shall [Valjean's] sins be forgiven," the answer is an unqualified yes because Valjean has sought forgiveness and practiced penitence. To refuse to forgive others is to choose to ignore the fact that God has forgiven the unforgivable in you. Here Javert is destroyed because he is "damned if [he'll] live in the debt of a thief," because he chooses to insulate himself behind the treacherously smothering nature of the theories with which he has aligned himself. Whereas Valjean's early life has brought about in him a sense of failure and a desire for revenge, it issues ultimately in penitence and, through his willingness to journey the "never-ending road to Calvary," becomes at the last an occasion for joy. On the other hand, Javert's sense of failure early and late leads to an overwhelming guilt and despondency. Hugo's contention is that the life lived for vengeance or in servitude to an inflexible and flawed legal code needs to be shattered in order that something better may be built. Such a shattering and re-building is the work of the Holy Spirit who "works like an acid on all complacency" (*Border Lands*, p. vii), who prepares the mansion of our souls into which Christ will come to dwell if we will but have it so.

The power of love, of Valjean's love explicitly in his release of Javert and his willingness to surrender, acts like an explosive which threatens to pulverize the fixed beliefs of the inspector which have led to his obsession with the law. Such a testimony to love and forgiveness affords Javert the opportunity to lose his life in order to find it, to abandon his obsession with the inflexible rigidity of the righteous law and accept instead the liberation that comes with the acceptance of grace. Though he has been robbed of his easy certainties, his obsessive convictions, and his reliance on a world defined by black and white, Javert will not repent because to do so means a change in direction, an attempt to take a clear look at his bearings and decide on a new path. He cannot face the fact that his good-intentioned self stinks because to do so would be painful and shocking. Thus it becomes impossible for him to say that "his righteousness is as filthy as rags" (*Yes to God*, p. 132).

Who Javert is as he jumps into the Seine is the consequence of choices made throughout his life, just as it will be with all of us. Those choices occur across the years in the history which is *Les Miserables*, within a temporal framework, but essentially they are the "timeless manifestations of the true desires of [the person who makes them]." To choose to ignore the reality of love when it is presented to us is to be imprisoned and if that choice is continued one ultimately rejects his own humanity because he rejects himself and others. The genius of the demonic is to make one despair and despair is what urges Javert to suicide. As Grossman notes, "Javert kills himself, quite simply, because he cannot deal with endlessly contemplating his intimate connection to both the world and others, that is, with trading his 'prosaic' nature for something more 'poetic'" (p. 107). That is despair.

Chapter 14

Seeing the Face of God:
To Love Another Person

In Charles Dickens's *Hard Times*, Thomas Gradgrind, a proponent of utilitarianism and a man described by the author as a "kind of canon loaded to the muzzle with facts" (p. 3), asks a young girl for the definition of a horse and she is unable to reply. Whatever knowledge she has is experiential, aesthetic, even intuitive, derived from her immersion in her father's occupation as a horse breaker. On the other hand, Bitzer, a young boy, is a veritable concatenation of facts about a horse, which he manages to spew out as if he were reciting the catechism. Dickens's point is that the mere accumulation of facts as the linchpin of life reduces what is majestically alive to something essentially inert. As Gradgrind discovers slowly and painfully, for the truth to be grasped only intellectually and as an accumulation of facts is for it to be rendered powerless to save. This is especially true of love, something that cannot be reduced to psychological constructs or a series of facts with arbitrarily defined limits as if it were a mathematical equation. Hugo's Bishop Myriel knows this well and his entire being is an extension of a simple principle, "love one another," and manifested outwardly "in a serene benevolence embracing all men and extending even beyond them" (p. 65). It is this that penetrates the callous Jean Valjean to the extent that the bishop becomes his spiritual guide. When truth seizes an individual in such a manner, his life takes on a spiritual dimension and an accompanying awareness that solidarity exists among men everywhere. This is what greets us at the end of *Les Miserables* and it is what is spread out before the reader-audience in a vast panoramic spectacle that is at the same time intensely personal.

The final scene of the novel and the musical returns us once again to the struggles first portrayed in "A tempest in a human skull." Like Javert, Valjean must now choose between "two roads which lay open to him, one seductive and the other terrifying" (p. 1142). What follows is a series of questions which tear at his soul and which make him aware intuitively that he is not living in a world where, as C. S. Lewis argues in the preface to *The Great Divorce*, "all roads are radii of a circle and where all, if followed long enough, will therefore draw gradually nearer and finally meet at the center" (pp. v-vi). The way of the Cross lies before him yet and, though he is on the road to the Kingdom of God, Hugo tells us, "Predestination does not always offer a straight road to the predestined" (p. 1142). All his life, Valjean has come up against rejection and fear, brutality and the menace of enslavement, even the imminence of death in the face of which he could apparently do nothing, and now there beckons "the abyss" (p. 1143). In the recollection of everything that has preceded, he becomes aware that "the first step [was] nothing; it is the last which [was] difficult" (p. 1143). The theft from Petit Gervais, Champmathieu, the prison ship Orion, the release of Javert, all pale before "Cosette's marriage and all that would ensue from it" (p. 1143). Yet always, in the midst of despair, in the emptiness of any moment, there is "the One who is present in the shadows" (p. 1144), the one who has promised that he will not leave us desolate, God. In the midst of Valjean's desert, God acts and in so doing equips Valjean to act.

When he determines to unmask himself before Marius, fittingly on Ash Wednesday, Valjean defines conscience for the young man as that which "thrusts you into a hell in which you feel the presence of God at your side. Your heart may be broken but you are at peace with yourself" (pp. 1150-1151). For him to tell his story of "slavery and shame" is not some sort of drastic remedy for a man who considers himself a desperate and grave sinner, nor is it, as Kenneth Leech remarks, "an extra devotion for the super pious or fastidious: it is [instead] a necessary element in every Christian's growth in prayer and life" (*True Prayer*, p. 131). For Valjean, his life, re-directed suddenly by the benevolence and compassion of the bishop, and growth, his movement toward wholeness in the naming of himself in the midst of severe trial and temptation, becomes more than just a series of spiritual experiences that have sparked a new existence. All those moments, including the confession to Marius, bring life itself, in its pain and joy, because Valjean has chosen to open himself to receive what they offer.

Though he does not know it as such, his confession to Marius is a kind of litany of penitence, a prayer in which he collects his past and acknowledges that "the time has come to journey on," to continue the pilgrimage. As T. S. Eliot notes in "Little Gidding,"

> And prayer is more
> Than an order of words, the conscious occupation
> of the praying mind, or the sound of the voice praying. (I, 46-48)

For Jean Valjean, the Holy Spirit of God continues to burn within him, to purge him, and when this moment takes place in the musical, when one does not have the leisurely luxury to re-read the passages, one can hear the old man speak from his heart so that what he confesses is not simply to Marius, but also to God. Implicit is the knowledge that the "way of love is cruciform, because love, to be true, must always carry within it the possibility of rejection" (*Passion for Pilgrimage*, p. 84), and rejection there will be.

In one sense, Marius is not there at all and Valjean's words, his prayer, transcend mere diction. As Allchin notes, it is as if the mind, here Valjean's mind, "is carried up through words beyond words, through time beyond time into a silence which is full of meaning and full of presence, full indeed of time, because it is the silence of an eternity, which is not the negation but the fulfillment of time" (*The Living Presence of the Past*, p. 113). As we read and as we listen to the music, much more is at work here than just having the mind assent to a spiritual necessity. The past is present to Valjean and to us, who have lived it with him, in a way that it is not to Marius and so even more of reality is conveyed, "more not less meaning than it did in the moment when it was itself 'present.' It is a past which is full of the riches of eternity" (p. 113). Valjean continues to empty himself of any tendency toward self-centeredness and thus his journey, nearing completion, will enable him to find ultimately that joy for which he was created. Because he seeks to do what he believes is pleasing to God, because he chooses to risk the traverse of a difficult terrain with all its doubts and challenges and crises, the rest of his life will be pure and holy so that "at the last [he will] come to [God's] eternal joy" (*The Book of Common Prayer*, p. 269).

In the last paragraph of the penultimate book, Hugo prepares the reader for the final scene in Valjean's room by noting the gradual extinguishing of his life.

> His expression seemed to say, 'What is the use?' There was no longer any light in his eyes, nor did the tears gather as formerly. But his head was still thrust forward, painfully revealing the folds in his thin neck. (p. 1172)

He has chosen freely to surrender what made him happy and it is apparent that he has prepared himself painfully for death by living a life of self-abandonment. He is able to approach that death with the unspoken certainty that to have given himself "away in love is the perfect satisfaction for which [he] crave[s]" and thus he is able to pray still for Cosette and Marius, now aware fully of the dangers of possessive love. In the surrender, in the realization that "she was never mine to keep," he relinquishes the last thing which he has tried to hold on to.

This prepares one for the final scene in Valjean's room, a scene which avoids excessive mawkishness and sentimentality because it is grounded so securely in theological truth. The same is true of the stage production which contains one of the most profoundly simple lyrics in Broadway musical history: "To love another person is to see the face of God." The setting on the stage mirrors precisely Hugo's description of Valjean's room and the nearness of death to its occupant.

The bishop's candlesticks were in their usual place on the mantelpiece; he got two wax candles out of a drawer and, putting them in the candlesticks, lighted them, although it was broad daylight. One may see candles lighted in rooms occupied by the dead. Every step he took, moving from one room to the other, exhausted him, and he had frequently to sit down and rest. It was not just a case of ordinary fatigue which uses up energy and recovers it; it was the last effort of which he was capable, exhausted life spending itself in an effort which it will not be able to repeat. (pp. 1176-1177)

What lies ahead immediately is Valjean's final redemption, indeed, his resurrection. This will remain for us a mystery that can only be lived and felt rather than articulated. It is the peculiar power of the music and Hugo's diction to make us feel and know.

Jean Valjean is alone: alone on the stage, alone "in the shadows," "alone at the end of the day," but alone in a different way than the wretched of the earth who are closer to death and deeper in debt at the end of their days. In his loneliness, bathed in the small light shed by the bishop's candlesticks, Jean Valjean is able to embrace death because he is turned toward God. In the reprise of "Bring Him Home," it is now Valjean who prays that he, rather than someone for whom he intercedes, be brought home, that is to his eternal home. To be taken to that place where God dwells renders physical death less frightening, even less relevant. The petition now provides the finishing brush strokes on a portrait begun years ago, a portrait constructed out of layers of experience, a portrait that was always in process as the journey was undertaken. The final stage of the journey is what Alan Jones refers to as "the pilgrimage to liberty" (*Journey Into Christ*, p. 123). As he has trod the way of the Cross, Valjean has stumbled, fallen, died to himself, and been re-born. He has journeyed so because he chose to respond to that notion of eternity that the bishop planted years ago, that simple yet overwhelmingly powerful idea that we are not quite at home here.

Valjean has died before he dies. Only because he has done this is he able to petition God as he does. The truth of his life, the dignity of how he has tried to live it, desperately at times, lies in his willingness to be answerable to God, to have learned to love him in the "patient working out in everyday affairs of what love that knows no limit will require" (*Yes to God*, p. 79). That Valjean can pray "take me now to thy care" is the end of a pilgrimage to what is really and truly real and the entire request expresses the truth of what someone said is the whole known in the part, the truth that is God and the part that is ours.

Just before that pilgrimage can be completed, as he sits in his room, Valjean is surrounded by a white light and we begin to see that his being, that which so marks him as human, is in the process of being exalted. Since his encounter with the bishop, Valjean has tried to act with justice, mercy, generosity, compassion, and love in his dealings with others. Now all that remains for him to complete his life is the presence of Cosette and this transpires as Marius discovers the truth about his father-in-law and expresses it succinctly—"Your father is a saint." In the novel, the recognition is more protracted and culminates in Marius' declaration that he and Cosette will not allow Valjean "to go on any more journeys" (p. 1194), that he now belongs to them. Marius begins to know the inherent truth of Peguy's observation that "when you love someone, you love him as he is, but that, in turn, depends upon taking trouble to face the revelation of what he is." Now he must learn as well that people do not belong to one. Such a lesson costs one, but the price is well paid because it leads to freedom finally rather than imprisonment, to one's true home rather than those earthly homes that confine.

When Valjean sings that he can now die in peace because his life is blessed, he echoes the novel.

> Jean Valjean had listened without hearing. He had listened to the music of her voice rather than to the words, and one of those great tears that are the deep pearls of the soul brimmed in his eye. He murmured:
>
> 'This is the proof that God is good...

The tear did not fall but lingered in his eye and he
replaced it with a smile. Cosette took his two hands in
hers.

'Your hands are so cold,' she said. 'Are you ill? Are you in
pain?'

'No,' said Valjean. 'I'm not in pain. Only – ' he broke off
again.

'Only what?'

'I'm going to die in a little while.' (p. 1195)

The peace at which he finally arrives is inward. It is intensified
and it is marked as an occasion for joy by Cosette's presence, but
the joy that is his is derived essentially from his surrender to and
union with God. It is "independent of circumstance." God most
certainly is good and to know this is to rest in the belief that life
eternal is God's gift to us mediated to us through his Son.

The grace of God is always free and unmerited, an offer that
one can choose to accept or reject. Valjean's decision to accept the
gift, to open it, and to respond to it exacts a price, but that price
issues ultimately in transfiguration, the completion of that to
which Hugo pointed early in the novel. Valjean illuminates what
John Baillie meant when he wrote about grace in *On Knowledge
of God*.

When I respond to God's call, the call is God's and the
response is mine; and yet the response is God's too; for not
only does He call me in His grace, but also by His grace
brings the response to birth within my soul. (*Concise
Dictionary of Religious Quotations*, p. 91)

The response within Valjean's soul has enabled him to become
a "fountain of love" (Grossman, p. 29) and it leads to his singing
"forgive me all my trespasses and take me to your glory." Such a plea
reflects an attitude now rooted deep within him, a commitment
born of the examination of all his motives and intentions—the theft
of bread and the candlesticks, the encounter with Petit Gervais,
the rescue of Champmathieu, the various engagements with

Javert, the journey to the barricades, the relinquishing of his hold on Cosette—and he acknowledges them to God. Indeed, it is more than a plea; it is a prayer. Precisely, it is a prayer of abandonment and, as Neuhaus notes in *Death on a Friday Afternoon*, it is in the "darkness of abandonment that God's power shines through our human weakness" (p. 136). Such desire for reconciliation and such a yearning for joy is a dynamic mixture and it explodes in the novel and on the stage. What Valjean grasps intuitively becomes also apparent to us and draws a response: at the center of any such experience, the fact of pardon is rooted. God has loved Valjean into fullness of being, transformed into goodness what was bent toward evil and on the road to Hell, and brought moral and spiritual life out of what was apparently dead. In essence, in the act of contrition which is followed by forgiveness, God acts to free Valjean and us, if we, too, will accept this gift which flows from God's decisive act on the Cross, "from bondage to the past so that we may live toward the future" (*Living Presence of the Past*, p. 35), wherever that immediate future may be, in this world or in the next. Martin Smith makes the point that it is on the Cross and through the empty tomb that one discovers God's explosive "yes to us, which cancels all our nos to God" (*Reconciliation*, p. 12). Valjean's prayer is a recognition of God's love affair with him and his desire to bring Valjean home.

My one major quibble with the musical is here at the end, at Valjean's death. In the novel, he is asked whether he needs a priest and his reply is that he already has one:

> "...and he pointed upwards as though there were some other being present whom he alone could see. Indeed it is not improbable that the bishop was present in those last moments of his life." (p. 1198)

In the eternal present, the bishop is present and time, simultaneously, collapses, explodes, and intersects as Valjean becomes one with the communion of saints, part of the "blessed company of all faithful people." On the stage, the bishop is absent, a missed opportunity to emphasize the theological depth of Valjean's journey. That

Fantine and Eponine are present suggests that Kretzmer is aware of the idea of the intersection of the timeless and time, of T. S. Eliot's speculation at the beginning of *Four Quartets*.

> Time present and time past
> Are both perhaps present in time future... (ll. 1-2)

For Valjean the mystic who can speak to the dead Fantine, temporal divisions in time become an illusion and all time for him becomes suddenly eternally present and links him to Christ in the Incarnation. Allchin is especially perceptive here.

> ...the moment of the intersection of the timeless and time, the moment when the eternal power of divine forgiveness and new life enters into the very heart of man, is a moment of such power that it can have effects backwards as well as forwards in time, turning the experience of loss into a new and deeper discovery of integrity.
> (*Living Presence of the Past*, p. 35)

And.

> ...all moments of the 'intersection of the timeless with time,' however fleetingly glimpsed are recognized as having the quality of incarnation in them, and are linked with the one Incarnation.
> (*Living Presence of the Past*, p. 36)

Valjean's vision of the bishop and his grasping of Fantine's hand validate his engagement in the actual everyday experience of men and women and when he sings "take me to your glory" we have set before us the beginning of a definition of heaven, an explicit affirmation of an implicit awareness that Valjean's future glory outweighs all his sufferings. Indeed, such glory is so much greater than any of the hardships of his life that it is hardly worthwhile to offer any comparison.

His prayer has indeed made its way heavenward and, as Ecclestone notes, since it does so "within the Yes of Christ, [it is] a yes that will not allow him to be wrenched away from God" (p. 12).

It is an "edge of glory" that is discovered to have always been there, calling to him by name in his dreams and yearnings so that to walk the "never-ending road to Calvary" is also to engage in that adventure which is "to walk the edge of glory" (*Border Lands*, p. ix). His journey Into Christ may now be perceived by all who have eyes to see and ears to hear for precisely what it is: "the secret of the universe, the music of the spheres, the rhythm of every human heart" (*Journey Into Christ*, p. 53). Jean Valjean re-reads his life with some sense of guilt and shame, but beyond that he re-reads it with gratitude and wonder and we are invited to participate. The portrait is in God's hands and because he has surrendered to the supreme artist the final words of the musical function as a great chorus on the steps of the new Eden. The epic of one man's deliverance, the recollection of all who have played their part in his drama of salvation, is acclaimed in the imperative reminder to the audience: "And remember the truth that once was spoken, To love another person is to see the face of God." These final lines show us what the love affair which is Valjean's life really is: an engagement with the Resurrection.

It is my contention that the end of the novel and the finale of the musical are a manifestation of God's glory, each a transfiguration of its own. The truth of God transfigures Valjean by coming to him in so many forms: Fantine, Cosette, Marius, the Bishop of Digne. And the light that bathes the stage associates them all with that glory which has accrued to Valjean and which has its origins in God. All the figures on the stage, suffused in light, show us the true colors of what really is and affirm that somehow, even mysteriously and incomprehensibly, all things point to glory. Thus do grace and glory and love triumph over all those things which try to say no to them so that at the end one is buried, as someone once wrote, in "an avalanche of grace."

"To love another person is to see the face of God" is a symphony of its own, a simple verbal and musical affirmation that it is possible for good to triumph through suffering and pain, that such triumph is itself redemptive. Here at the close of the musical Valjean experiences the presence of Christ not as some sort of resuscitated corpse, but through his engagement with the living and the dead. In a phrase of Herbert O'Driscoll's, such an experience is "a grace beyond therapy" (*Prayers for the Breaking of Bread*, p. 36), a subtle proclamation that before Valjean had done anything, Christ had already done it at the cost of his human life. C. S. Lewis supplements this perception with the following observation from his essay "Christianity and Literature."

> Our whole destiny seems to lie in the opposite direction, in being as little as possible ourselves, in acquiring a fragrance that is not our own but borrowed, in becoming clear mirrors filled with the image of a face that is not ours. (p. 7)

Thus here at the end death doesn't quite matter to Valjean as it would have earlier. It happens to him but it is a beginning, not an end, an entrance rather than an exit.

In his commentary on John's Gospel, William Temple illuminates this theological point when he cites from *Doctrine in the Church of England.*

> The Resurrection (of Jesus Christ) has made possible for Christians a new interpretation of the facts of death and mortality....Death becomes not a mere gateway to be passed through, nor the mere casting away of a perishable body, but a loss which is turned into a gain, a giving up of life which is made the means whereby that life is received back again, renewed, transfigured, and fulfilled. (*Readings in John's Gospel*, p. 169)

The aged Valjean, the weakened and dying Valjean, is also the transfigured Valjean. That he can arrive at a moment when he can verbalize that he was foolish to believe that things belonged to him, that the Thenardiers, wicked though they were, must be forgiven, and that he can recall Fantine into a present memory for Cosette shows the impact of God upon him. For Valjean, God is the given in all equations, the one "who watches us all from above and knows what he is doing amid his splendid stars" (p. 1200). Remembering the bishop who lived his life in the phrase from the Gospel of John, "love one another," Valjean affirms this moral and spiritual imperative which he has tried to live out in his life and says to Marius and Cosette "Love one another always." It is in this injunction, spoken with tenderness, that his last word is uttered, but that last word remains a present reality to those who read it and to those who listen carefully to the musical affirmation that "to love another person is to see the face of God."

One of the miracles of the Christian Gospel is that in the midst of despair and pain one can always find the presence of joy. In *The Pilgrim's Regress*, C. S. Lewis has God say to John the pilgrim that "for this end I made your senses and for this end your imagination, that you might see my face and live." In a wonderful song of renewal by Bob Dufford, SJ, *"Be Not Afraid,"* one discovers the truth expressed in Isaiah that barren deserts and raging waters, burning flames and the power of hell, the insults of the wicked and the presence of death at one's side will not hinder one from seeing the face of God and living because God has gone before us and his love will carry the day. At the end of his journey into the mystery of love, into Christ, into that stillness which is God, Jean Valjean is liberated and what we see finally at the end of his journey is a kind of transfigured ascension.

When T. S. Eliot wrote in "Little Gidding that

> the communication
> Of the dead is tongued with fire beyond the language of
> the living.
> Here, the intersection of the timeless moment
> Is England and nowhere. Never and always. (ll. 50-53)

He certainly did not anticipate the musical version of *Les Miserables*. However, I think that it is a stroke of genius on the part of those responsible for the musical production to end with all the dead from Valjean's past joining with him to surround Marius and Cosette and sing the reprise of "Do You Hear the People Sing?" How often, I wonder, has the audience risen en masse at the conclusion of this number to applaud the vision, not just the performance. Perhaps the transfiguration is palpably present, the recognition that all claims to egotism have been relinquished a verifiable fact, and the steps taken by the dead, hands joined, toward us function as a beacon that beckons us into the future. Yes, there is a world beyond the barricades which one longs to see; yes, one can "live again in freedom in the garden of the Lord"; yes, one can climb to the light and know that "the darkest night will end and the sun will rise"; and yes, heaven is the real reality, the place of ultimate freedom where one is loosed from one's chains and grief and death are swallowed up in joy.

The dead on the stage make it possible for us to see the true destination of all creation, a creation lifted up and restored in Christ, a glimpse "of the glory of God which is to be revealed." In the "garden of the Lord," all the "fragments of our scattered existence come together at last and forever" (*Death on a Friday Afternoon*, p. 40). The new Paris, the transcendent Paris, is not merely a touched up copy of the old Paris earlier in the play; it is not that words to a song have been merely changed. Rather, it is just the reverse; it is the old which was the imperfect copy of the real that has always existed. Marius and Cosette, yet alive, can know this only imperfectly, but the small spark, the faint glimmer of absolute reality, perceived by them, perhaps even for the first time, in terms of its true nature can be the catalyst for them on their journey and for us on ours. That this "blessed communion, fellowship divine" appears at the end opens us to what is beyond history, to what frees us "from the servitude of history" (*Living Presence of the Past*, p. 115).

The communion of saints on stage at the end cannot be discerned by either geography or canonization, but by that gracious attitude of offering, thanksgiving, remembering, and supplication which takes place as one joins his voice with the "Angels and Archangels and with all the company of heaven." Here we discover imaginatively the truth of Saint Paul's belief that "the last enemy to be destroyed is death" (I Cor. 15:26) and those on stage share in the risen life of Christ. The joy that awaits them as they move "further up and further in" is qualitative and not quantitative; it lies beyond "all present mortal anticipations." We discover here in the Finale that, by the supreme act of his creative love, God will show that all that is past can be altered and all things brought to fulfillment in him. Since we, too, intersect with the living and the dead, the time-bound and the timeless, we have revealed for us the

> ...unmeasured possibilities of love and knowledge of joy and compassion, capacities of constructive action and creative work, which lie hidden in the heart and mind of man, and which are liberated when the heart and mind are opened to God and touched by the action of his grace.
>
> (*Living Presence of the Past*, p. 99)

At the end, in the power of choral music and song, the past is present to us in all its dimensions, but now it is a past present in such a way that it "conveys more not less reality, more not less meaning than it did in the moment when it was itself 'present'" (*Living Presence of the Past*, p. 113). In this moment, it is possible, if we are well tuned, to hear the Word beyond the words, to know that song which resounds throughout the universe and lies within every human being waiting to burst out. Read and heard properly, *Les Miserables* ends with the sound of triumphant laughter in heaven because we have begun "to drink joy from the fountain of joy" (*The Weight of Glory*). As Augustine wrote, "we shall rest and we shall see, we shall see and we shall love, we shall love and we shall praise."

BIBLIOGRAPHY

Adam, David. 2000. *The Best of David Adam's Celtic Vision*. Franklin, Wisconsin: Sheed and Ward.

_____. 2000. *Glimpses of Glory: Prayers for the Church Year*. Harrisburg, Pennsylvania: Morehouse.

Allchin, A. M. 1981. *The Living Presence of the Past: The Dynamics of Christian Tradition*. New York: Seabury.

_____. 1988. *Participation in God: A Forgotten Strand in Anglican Tradition*. London: Darton, Longman and Todd.

Allen, Diogenes. 1987. *Love: Christian Romance, Marriage, Friendship*. Cambridge, Massachusetts: Cowley.

Behr, Edward. 1989. *The Complete Book of Les Miserables*. New York: Little, Brown.

Bloom, Alan. 1987. *The Closing of the American Mind*. New York: Simon and Schuster.

Bonhoeffer, Dietrich. 1995. *The Cost of Discipleship*. New York: Simon and Schuster.

Dickens, Charles. 1987. *Hard Times*. New York: Oxford University Press.

Ecclestone, Alan. 1975. *Yes to God*. London: Darton, Longman and Todd.

Eliot, T. S. 1971. *The Four Quartets*. New York: Harcourt Brace Jovanovich.

Friedman, Thomas L. 2000. *The Lexus and the Olive Tree: Understanding Globalization*. New York: Anchor Books.

Grossman, Elizabeth. 1996. *Les Miserables: Conversion, Revolution, Redemption*. New York: Twayne.

Herbert, George. 1974. 'The Elixir.' In *The English Poems of George Herbert*, ed. C. A. Patrides, 188. London: Darton, Longman and Todd.

Hugo, Victor. 1982. *Les Miserables*. Trans. Norman Denny. New York: Penguin.

Jones, Alan. 1989. *Passion for Pilgrimage: Notes for the Journey Home*. New York: Harper and Row.

_____. 1992. *Journey Into Christ*. Boston: Cowley.

Leech, Kenneth. 1995. *True Prayer*. Harrisburg, Pennsylvania: Morehouse.

Lewis, C. S. 1944. *The Pilgrim's Regress*. New York: Sheed and Ward.

_____. 1963. *Letters to Malcolm: Chiefly on Prayer*. New York: Harcourt, Brace and World.

_____. 1974. *Mere Christianity*. New York: Macmillan.

_____. 1996. *The Problem of Pain*. New York: Simon and Schuster.

_____. 1979. 'Die Audiendis Poetis.' In *Studies in Medieval and Renaissance Literature*, 1-17. Cambridge: Cambridge University Press.

_____. 1960. *The Four Loves*. New York: Harcourt, Brace and Company.

_____. 1970. 'Man or Rabbit.' In *God in the Dock: Essays on Theology and Ethics*, 108-113. Grand Rapids Michigan: William B. Eerdmanns.

_____. 1967. 'Christianity and Literature.' In *Christian Reflections*, 1-11. Grand Rapids, Michigan: William B. Eerdmanns.

_____. 1946. *The Great Divorce*. New York: Macmillan.

_____. 1956. *Till We Have Faces*. New York: Harcourt Brace Jovanovich.

Mascall, E. L. 1961. *Grace and Glory*. Harrisburg, Pennsylvania: Morehouse.

Muir, Edwin. 1960. 'The Transfiguration.' In *Edwin Muir: Collected Poems*, 198-200. London: Faber and Faber.

Neuhaus, Richard John. 2000. *Death on a Friday Afternoon*. New York: Basic Books.

O'Driscoll, Herbert. 1991. *Prayers for the Breaking of Bread: Meditations on the Collects of the Church Year*. Boston: Cowley.

Saint-Exupery, Antoine. 1971. *The Little Prince*. New York: Harcourt Brace Jovanovich.

Temple, William. 1955. *Readings in St. John's Gospel*. London: Macmillan.

Tolstoy, Leo. 1960. 'The Death of Ivan Ilych.' In 'The Death of Ivan Ilych and Other Stories,* Trans. Aylmer Maude and J. D. Duff, 95-156, New York: New American Library.

Traherne, Thomas. 1983. *Centuries of Meditation.* Harrisburg, Pennsylvania: Morehouse.

Williams, Charles. 1996. *Descent Into Hell.* Grand Rapids, Michigan: William B. Eerdmanns.

Williams, H. A. 1977. *Becoming What I Am.* London: Darton, Longman and Todd.

_____. 1979. *The Joy of God.* Springfield, Illinois: Templegate.

_____. 1975. *True Christianity.* Springfield, Illinois: Templegate.

_____. 1972. *True Resurrection.* Springfield, Illinois: Templegate.

_____. 1982. *The True Wilderness.* New York: Crossroad.

About the Author

The Rev. John E Morrison, III is an Episcopal priest and a retired English teacher. He holds degrees from Dartmouth College, Hofstra University, and the State University of New York at Stony Brook. He lives in Brightwaters, New York with his wife Susan.

Other Zossima Press Titles

C. S. Lewis

C. S. Lewis: Views From Wake Forest
Michael Travers, editor

Contains sixteen scholarly presentations from the international C. S. Lewis convention in Wake Forest, NC. Walter Hooper shares his important essay "Editing C. S. Lewis," a chronicle of publishing decisions after Lewis' death in 1963. Other contributors include James Como and Sanford Schwartz.

"Scholars from a variety of disciplines address a wide range of issues. The happy result is a fresh and expansive view of an author who well deserves this kind of thoughtful attention." Diana Pavlac Glyer, author of *The Company They Keep: C. S. Lewis and J.R.R. Tolkien as Writers in Community*.

Why I Believe in Narnia:
33 Essays & Reviews on the Life & Work of C. S. Lewis
By James Como

Chapters range from reviews of critical books, documentaries and movies to evaluations of Lewis' books to biographical analysis. In addition to close-up looks, Como reflects on the "big picture" of the most important contributions Lewis has made, not just in literature, but as a social philosopher and reformer. An invaluable tool for appreciating the breadth and depth of Lewis' thinking.

"A valuable, wide-ranging collection of essays by one of the best informed and most astute commentators on Lewis' work and ideas." Peter Schakel, author *Imagination & the Arts in C. S. Lewis*

The Library Jack Built:
A Comprehensive Listing of C. S. Lewis' Personal Library
By Roger White *(January 2010 publication)*

This book traces the dispersal of C. S. Lewis' personal library following his death in 1963. The acquisition history is detailed and the books are listed. User-friendly bibliographic listing is coded by collection location and presented in two forms: first alphabetically by author and then grouped by subject. Two appendices are included that list books originally in, or believed to have been in, Lewis' library that are currently unaccounted for in terms of location, owner, or provenance. Devotees and scholars of Lewis will appreciate *The Library that Jack Built* for the insight it provides into the books that captured and shaped this much loved and influential man.

George MacDonald

Diary of an Old Soul & The White Page Poems
George MacDonald and Betty Aberlin

In 1880, George MacDonald, the Scottish poet, novelist and preacher, published *A Book of Strife in the Form of the Diary of an Old Soul*. The first edition of this book of daily poems included a blank page opposite each page of poems. Readers were invited to write their own reflections on the "white page." MacDonald wrote: "Let your white page be ground, my print be seed, growing to golden ears, that faith and hope may feed." Betty Aberlin responded to MacDonald's invitation with daily poems of her own.

Betty Aberlin's close readings of George MacDonald's verses and her thoughtful responses to them speak clearly of her poetic gifts and spiritual intelligence. Luci Shaw, poet

George MacDonald: Literary Heritage and Heirs
Roderick McGillis

It has been 15 years since Roderick McGillis edited *For the Childlike*, a landmark collection of essays about George MacDonald's writings. This latest collection of 14 essays sets a new standard that will influence MacDonald studies for many more years. George MacDonald experts are increasingly evaluating his entire corpus within the nineteenth century context. This volume provides further evidence that MacDonald will eventually emerge from the restrictive and somewhat misleading reputation of being C. S. Lewis' spiritual "master."

This comprehensive collection represents the best of contemporary scholarship on George MacDonald. Rolland Hein, author of *George MacDonald: Victorian Mythmaker.*

In the Near Loss of Everything:
George MacDonald's Son in America
Dale Wayne Slusser

In the summer of 1887, George MacDonald's son Ronald, newly engaged to artist Louise Blandy, sailed from England to America to teach school. The next summer he returned to England to marry Louise and bring her back to America. On August 27, 1890, Louise died leaving him with an infant daughter. Ronald once described losing a beloved spouse as "the near loss of everything". Dale Wayne Slusser unfolds this poignant story with unpublished letters and photos that give readers a glimpse into the close-knit MacDonald family. Also included is Ronald's essay about his father, *George MacDonald: A Personal Note*, plus a selection from Ronald's 1922 fable, *The Laughing Elf*, about the necessity of both sorrow and joy in life.

Harry Potter

Harry Potter & Imagination:
The Way Between Two Worlds
Travis Prinzi

"What we achieve inwardly will change outer reality." Those words, written by Plutarch and quoted by J.K. Rowling her 2008 Harvard commencement speech, sum up both the importance of the *Harry Potter* series and the argument of Travis Prinzi's analysis of the best-selling books in *Harry Potter & Imagination: The Way Between Two Worlds*. Imaginative literature places a reader between two worlds: the story world and the world of daily life, and challenges this reader to imagine and to act for a better world. Starting with discussion of Harry Potter's more important themes, *Harry Potter & Imagination* takes readers on a journey through the transformative power of those themes for both the individual and for culture by placing Rowling's series in its literary, historical, and cultural contexts.

Deathly Hallows Lectures
John Granger

In *The Deathly Hallows Lectures*, John Granger reveals the finale's brilliant details, themes and meanings. Even the most ardent of *Harry Potter* fans will be surprised by and delighted with the Granger's explanations of the three dimensions of meaning in *Deathly Hallows*. Ms. Rowling has said that alchemy sets the "parameters of magic" in the series; after reading the chapter-length explanation of *Deathly Hallows* as the final stage of the alchemical Great Work, the serious reader will understand how important literary alchemy is in understanding Rowling's artistry and accomplishment.

Repotting Harry Potter:
A Professor's Book-by-Book Guide for the Serious Re-Reader
James Thomas

A professor of literature for over thirty years, Dr. James W. Thomas takes us on a tour through the *Potter* books in order to enjoy them in different ways upon subsequent readings. Re-readers will be pleasantly surprised at what they may have missed in the books and at what secrets Rowling has hidden for us to uncover as we revisit these stories. The professor's informal discussions focus on puns, humor, foreshadowing, literary allusions, narrative techniques, and other aspects of the *Potter* books that are hard-to-see on the hurried first or fifth reading. Dr. Thomas's light touch proves that a "serious" reading of literature can be fun.

Printed in the United States
218524BV00001B/5/P

9 780972 322195